Under the Sign of the Lily

The Messianic Sophianic Age

God Wants the Best for You

*The Eternal Word,
the One God, the Free Spirit,
speaks through Gabriele,
as through all the prophets of God—
Abraham, Job, Moses, Elijah, Isaiah,
Jesus of Nazareth,
the Christ of God*

GOD
Wants the Best for You

Your Companion Through the Year

by Gabriele

Gabriele
Publishing House

"God Wants the Best for You"

First Edition, November 2022
© Gabriele-Verlag Das Wort GmbH
Max-Braun-Str. 2, 97828 Marktheidenfeld
www.gabriele-verlag.com
www.gabriele-publishing-house.com

Translated from the original German title:

„Gott möchte für Dich das Beste"

The German edition is the work of reference
for all questions regarding the meaning of the contents.

All rights reserved

Order No. S331en

All decorative letters: © Gabriele-Verlag Das Wort

Printed by: KlarDruck GmbH, Marktheidenfeld, Germany

ISBN 978-3-96446-371-5

*Be still—God dwells in you.
God goes with me into the day;
God is with me at every hour,
at every moment.
God wants the best for me.*

January 1

God's help is in all things

Your new day reveals itself to you in many situations and in many moments, in the pleasant ones and the not so pleasant ones. However, your day brings you only what you have input in this incarnation or in previous incarnations—thus, your sinfulness that you have not yet cleared up and worked off.

Dear brother, dear sister, no matter what your day brings to you—one thing is certain: God's help is in all things, because God, the omnipresent power of our Father, is in everything and with everyone—also with you. There is nothing that would be outside of God. God is in everyone and everything the power that vivifies everything and streams through everything. God is help, love and guidance.

January 2

Self-mastery begins with self-observation

The path to the eternal Self begins with the mastery of oneself through the power of the Christ of God. We master our life only with the power of Christ. If we do not let our life just pass by in egocentric, human thinking and the corresponding actions, but instead endeavor to look behind our own façade, by pausing frequently and asking ourselves: "What is actually happening now? What am I thinking, how am I feeling, what am I reacting to?" then we take the step out of superficiality.

In this self-observation, we will become aware of many things about ourselves. We will discover many a thing that we were not aware of before. Then the question comes up: Do we want to stay the way we presently are, or do we want to change? Then our life will come alive, and we have the chance that things will get better.

January 3

Pause, and ask God for help

If we frequently make ourselves aware in the situations and moments of the day that God's help is in everyone and in everything, then it will be easier and easier for us to briefly pause in a situation to ask for God's help. Then we can feel His presence. It is also possible that the help comes directly. Then we are happy about it and feel that our hearts are linked with God, our Father.

Go into this new day gladly and confidently and, if you would like to—for we all have free will—every now and then realize that God is always with you, with all people. God is always the help. He never turns away from you; He is always *for* you.

January 4

Every thought is energy that is not lost

Similar to a farmer who plants the seeds in the soil in autumn, we plant our seeds in the field of our life, in our soul. Every thought is a seed corn. After a certain time of maturation, a seedling springs forth that can become a plant or a tree. The positive seed produces good fruit; the negative fruit produces the fruits of its kind—according to what lies in the seed corn.

What goes out from us that is positive and that is negative also goes into our soul as a seed corn as well as into the atmosphere and the stars and planets, which store our feelings, sensations, thoughts, words and actions as energy.

The harvest time will come one day, and we will receive what we have sown.

January 5

Make God, your heavenly Father, happy!

Realize that One always loves you: God, your and our Father. He wants your thoughts to correspond to His heavenly Order. What do you want?

God, your Father, our Father, is closer to you than you can imagine. He wants the best for you. He wants you to be happy and joyful. Make Him, your heavenly Father, happy. Overcome the bad and tormenting thoughts with the power of Christ, who dwells in you. Clear up what your thoughts radiate to you, and affirm the law of love, from which you fulfill another spiritual principle again today.

January 6

Expect nothing, and surrender to God

What do you expect? What do you expect of the present day, of this year, for instance? What do you expect of people and situations?

Often we expect something that is, so we think, good and beneficial for us. Especially when we expect something, it does not happen. But when we give what we desire over to God and let His will prevail, then many a thing comes to us unexpectedly.

We could resolve for today: "Expect nothing; surrender yourself to God," or: "surrender yourself to the will of God." If we stay aware of this, then suddenly we feel inner stillness, inner strength and a certain sense of security: God wants the best for us.

January 7

The good seed opens up undreamed possibilities

If our good seed sprouts—and it will sprout, because nothing is lost—then things will go better for us from day to day. Things will come toward us that we have not imagined until now. Situations will be solved that we thought were insolvable. Strength will be given to us that we did not know until now as a human being.

Get going, dear brother, dear sister, let us analyze the bad aspects that we have recognized in ourselves!

The day has not yet ended ...

January 8

Experience: God is there!

It is a great help for us to realize again and again in the situations that confront us, in the moments of our day that God's help is in everyone and in everything.

What we address in our thoughts intensifies in us. If we turn to God again and again, then the living communication with Him builds up more and more.

If you want to, try it; in everything that you encounter, ask God for His help. Go consciously with God and you will sense: God's help, His love, is always with you. He is always there for you, indeed, for all of us, and can help.

January 9

Look for the good in everything, and you will find it

Look for the positive in the negative and you will find it! Look for the positive also in your fellow people whom you encounter, and you will find that your neighbor has many good characteristics.

Become a discoverer of the good, and you will gain completely new and undreamt-of aspects in your life. Good aspects! Your positive attitude will help you to remain composed and to find a way or the next step. If you want to, try it!

Each day is a chance to find the good in everything.

January 10

Right decisions
ease the heart

*Y*our stirrings and movements are reflected, in turn, in your thoughts. They can be thoughts in God, but also human, egocentric thoughts, thoughts of belittlement, envy, anxiety and the like. What will you do with your thoughts?

Sinfulness forces us again and again to make a decision. Either we clear up what our thoughts point out to us or we expand our sinfulness. If we clear it up, it will become easier, if we move the negative, it will become harder.

If you have made the right decision during the day, then in the evening your heart is at ease. Put everything that moved you into God's kind hands—and yourself, too. He loves you and knows you. He stands by you. He carries you through the night and will be your companion again tomorrow.

January 11

The belief in God's guidance is not fulfilled by being passive

Many a one says, "God's guidance in my life?—You have to believe this and grow stronger in your belief." This is correct when we are talking solely about belief.

When it is merely an acquired, denominational teaching that says: Just believe, then everything will take care of itself—we will also fail with the first test in our life and will doubt God. Then we will doubt His kindness, because this belief, that everything will be good without our doing anything, will not be fulfilled; for: The true belief is an active one.

January 12

Experience what it means to strive higher. Fulfill your prayers

*B*egin the day with God. Fill your soul and your whole body with your deep breath. Stand at the window. Breathe in and out deeply. Watch your breathing and look toward heaven. Whatever you see—sun or clouds—whatever you feel—rain or wind—God's breath is in everything. Accept the elemental forces just as they show themselves to you today, then you will also accept the great Creator-power in you, which breathes through you—in and out, in and out.

If you feel that your breathing is calm and deep, if you are automatically breathing deeply, then stay in this deep breathing, and you will recognize that you already do all your morning tasks more calmly.

If you would like to, go into a meditative prayer afterward. Pray from your heart. Let the prayer thoughts come via your deep breathing and you will experience that your soul is infinitely thankful, for it can now express itself through you. It can now pray from the heart through you, the human being, and, at the same time, convey to you what it asks of you, namely, that you fulfill your prayers, so that it can pray through you in an ever deeper and more God-filled way.

Through a deep, meditative prayer, your sight opens for more beautiful and finer vibrations.

January 13

Speak consciously!

To grow closer to the Inner Light means to be silent more and more—not only to externally close your mouth, but to cultivate pure, divine thoughts.

People who always speak out what they think will not find their way to inner stillness. They talk and talk and talk. And those who constantly talk will gradually become careless in their speaking. Others can easily deal with such a person.

Therefore, resolve to speak with concentration and to speak what you say from the truth, that is, to express only what is true and that has no secondary tones, that is, side thoughts.

January 14

To act makes you free

During the day, especially at noontime and in the evening, let us turn frequently to God, our Father, and thank Him for everything, whether it was good or less good! In true gratitude lies devotion to God. In this devotion, we attain the strength to rejoice in the good, but also to clear up with Christ what is not good and to do good in the future.

We cannot leave the doing to someone else. Dear brother, dear sister, to act makes you free. A strong thought of courage, a push—and you will clear up what the day brought you that was not good and that upset you. Now breathe deeply and look at the positive. Breathe it into you and be glad. Consciously take in this joy—it is the Lord's love radiation in you. Take this peace and happiness further with you.

January 15

Vigor according to God's commandments through active faith

The true faith is the active faith, the inner experience that God exists in us, that He wants only the best for us and gives us the strength to make the best of the situations of our existence. This then brings the inner certainty in every ordeal of our life.

Each day, no matter what comes to us, active faith helps us to clear up with Christ our agitations, which are indications of sinfulness, and to no longer do them. Through this active mastering of the tasks and difficulties with the power of the Christ of God, a spiritual dynamism develops, a being flooded by the inner life force and thus vigor according to God's commandment.

January 16

Have courage! The day wants to be your good friend

If you awakened today with good and uplifting thoughts, then in looking back, you will realize that you closed yesterday well, that your evening was mostly harmonious, that you also took the steps of clearing things up before sleep overcame you.

Have courage! The day always wants to be your good friend. It brings you only your own aspects and only as much as you are able to work off today.

January 17

The awareness of God's presence brings clarity and the sensitivity of your conscience

Know that through the affirmation "God helps us. He is always for and with us. He is here for each and every one, always present," the clear feeling for the good, the divine is awakened and strengthened in us. Likewise, on the other hand, we recognize the non-divine more quickly and in finer nuances, the base human aspects, so that we leave them behind us step by step and can make the best of our life.

With this exercise "God helps each one. God is always *for* us, always with us," you learn to distinguish ever better the egocentric from the selfless. Through this, your conscience becomes more sensitive, so that you are more certain in your decisions, because then in everything that you do, with each decision you will include God. And God helps!

January 18

The decision for God makes you free

If you like, think about truth and deception, that is, illusion. Truth is also clarity and decisiveness. Those who are truthful will clearly recognize what is good and right and will also act according to their clear recognitions. A clear decision challenges you to be a person of action in the law of God.

The decision for God makes you free and brings you closer to God. If you continue to cling to deception, to illusion, then you will also be deceived. If we let ourselves be deceived, then we do not know ourselves and will soon also be disappointed and resigned. Everyone receives what they have input according to their way of feeling, thinking, speaking and acting.

Be decisive and act.

January 19

Put in order what stands between you and your fellow people

Do not let difficulties between you and your neighbor wait too long to be dealt with. If you want to, recognize your part and clear it up. For the path of clearing things up, the following Christian principles apply: Repent with all your heart of the sins you have recognized. Ask for forgiveness. Forgive your neighbor, too. Make amends for what you may have caused and no longer commit this sinfulness.

If, for instance, you realize that you were not so friendly toward your colleagues at work—you notice this with your uncertainty and restlessness—then know: Now is the chance to put this in order.

God never turns away from you. Ask Him, and He will help you. Real, deep remorse and clearing things up in our thoughts helps—and is a good resolution for the coming time.

January 20

Everything good starts with the movement of your heart

If you like, take the following sentence into your world of thoughts: All changes toward the good first take place in a person's heart.
Ask God, that He may help you in everything that the day brings. You know that God is in us, and He always helps—because He loves you, because He loves us, because He loves all people, all souls, all Being. Indeed, He loves all Being, because He is the love.

January 21

God's all-wise powers will be active in your plan, provided your intentions are in the will of the Eternal One

*I*f you like, look into the demands of the coming day, make a plan and place this in the hands of your eternal Father.

The inputs of your plan are energies that begin already now to have an effect on their realization and fulfillment. It is God's all-wise powers that become active for you, provided your intentions are in the will and the law of the Eternal.

January 22

Closing the day in the evening and a good plan prepare the new day. Thankfulness awakens more positive powers

If we closed the day well during the previous evening and planned the following one well, then the day has been prepared and awaits us; and we wake up feeling calm and confident.

Out of the tranquility of the night and the freshness of the morning hour, perhaps you feel the need to thank God, your Father, who gives you this day. Gratitude awakens more positive powers and strengthens the connection to the One who is the source of strength and life and who wants to consciously accompany you through the day.

January 23

Stay true to yourself; find peace in yourself

If, for the most part, we stay true to ourselves, to our life plan, we will go through our day alertly and allow self-recognition to be followed by overcoming ourselves. If we clear things up, we feel how happy and free this makes us!

Bring to mind again and again your precepts, your plan for life and faithfulness; read it to yourself calmly and reflectively. Then you will recognize where there may still be something to clarify, to clear up.

We should catch every unpleasant thought and not put aside anything unfinished. Grasp it and in your feelings and sensations recognize what it wants to tell you. Then you can clear it up with Christ, so that you find your way into peace and inner tranquility.

JANUARY 24

The brief, heartfelt prayer—a help for coping with your day

If after your morning prayer, you have already looked more closely at the thoughts that move you, then after getting dressed you will again go into a brief and heartfelt prayer. A suggestion, a help for you: Go into a prayer meditation, by accompanying every prayer thought with your feelings and sensations and, if possible, letting it become a picture. The prayer-picture then goes into your conscious mind, so that you can master the morning and the whole day out of the power of prayer.

The help is there: Christ in you. Always be aware that you can go to Christ in you at any time. Be aware that Christ should be the center of your life. If you put Christ before all things, then your day will be more powerful and you will master your day's work with His power.

January 25

Alignment with our center, Christ, gives strength to solve many a thing

Burdening thoughts upon awakening? Direct them away from you; determine that they wait until you have linked with God, your Lord, in you. A heartfelt prayer of thanks in the morning brings us the alignment with our center—Christ. If we orient our life toward the fulfillment of the commandments of God, toward His law, by striving to do His will, we will go through our days aware that He accompanies us through the day.

If the thoughts speak to you again, then you have the strength—for example, with the little word "why"—to get to the bottom of them, to ask where they come from and what you can initiate so that many a thing is resolved and you become free. Important is that, right away, you follow your recognition with clearing them up and that you know how you will now act.

January 26

It is your responsibility to fulfill what the day shows you

Each of us is responsible for whether we manage to keep peace with our neighbor. We ourselves are responsible for whether we manage to do good work, to recognize the meaning of our existence and to fulfill what the day shows us. We have the commandments of God and the teachings of the Sermon on the Mount, on which we can measure what we do or don't do. And Christ, our Redeemer, our Helper and Advisor, is always present! He is ready.

January 27

Go through the day consciously and close it consciously with Christ

God, your Father and the Father of us all, loves you, loves all of us. He wants the best for you. He wants you to go through the day consciously.
Close the day consciously with Christ in the evening.
May I give you some advice? If you feel restless, then in the evening do not go right away to your family, to your relatives, to your friends and acquaintances. Go to a quiet place where you can think once more about the day that is drawing to a close. Let the hours of the day pass through your consciousness so that you may recognize what made you calm or restless. Once more, you experience how you spoke or acted. Now clear up what made you restless—either through Christ or via Christ with your neighbor—then you will become calm.

January 28

God's Father-love—
the guiding ray into the Father's house

We are all united in God. No matter which path we still take—God loves us in His heart. And because He loves us, He radiates His Father-love—and one day we will cling to this glorious ray of love, which will then become the guiding ray into the Father's house.

If we do more and more what God wants, then we feel the inner happiness and the peace of person and soul. You will possibly say: "It is a long way to achieve that." I say to you: Those who want to and act accordingly will also achieve it shortly.

January 29

Could you stand before the face of God?

There are many points that we don't want to look at during the day, which, however, torment us or make us restless. Do not say: "I don't mind that. The whole world thinks, speaks or acts like me." Are you an imitator, or do you want to change the world a little bit toward the positive?

A small aid: If you were to now suddenly stand before the face of God, could you stand before Him without fear, without a bad feeling or without remorse? You may say: "I would have a bad feeling. Perhaps I would be overcome with remorse."

Recognize, dear brother, dear sister, whatever we would not want to have before the face of God, we should also refrain from before our fellow people, because God is in each one of our neighbors.

January 30

Write down your good resolution, as a help for doing it better in the future

If during the day you can overcome some things that are not nice, then you will also do it better in the future. Often it is useful to write down a good resolution, so that we can read it again and again, and be able to correct our course when we fall back into old habits.

January 31

Affirm the good in you and in your neighbor

"The other one is to blame!"—"The other one" is also a child of the light. The good in them is a part of you. Affirm the good also in your neighbor and know: What bothers you about them or even upsets you is, above all, in you yourself.

Clear up your base self, in order to achieve the high self, the divine, which will bring you joy and security. If we clear up our debit side, then more understanding for our fellow people will awaken in us. Our neighbor will no longer rub us the wrong way so often, because above all, we thereby recognize our own rough edges—our debit side.

By clearing things up, the being against one another diminishes as well as our difficulties. The gain is being for one another and a peaceful with one another as brothers and sisters.

FEBRUARY 1

God is the infinite kindness and love; He is the good

Many people complain about their suffering and a deplorable existence. They blame God for their condition; but God is the infinite goodness and love, He is the good. God is good. There is nothing bad in His law. Therefore, only good comes from Him, because God is good. Our sufferings, our sorrowful existence and our blows of fate come from our egoism, from our negative thinking and behavior. How often do we analogously think, "If the Kingdom of God is in us, then the Redeemer, the Christ of God, is also in us. Why doesn't He help?"

The Christ of God, our Redeemer, can deliver us from our suffering, hardship, illness and sorrow only if we want this, if we become aware of our filiation and do what is ultimately our true nature, our origin: to fulfill the law of God and the love for our neighbor.

February 2

The path to true recognition

Take note for the new day: The path to true recognition, which is, at the same time, the path to God, does not go through external leaders; it does not go through priests, pastors or other dignitaries, regardless of the title they hold.

The path to true recognition goes through your true self, which you grow closer to when you immerse yourself in your divine being, which is within you, and sincerely ask for help and support.

The true leader who knows your path to God is Christ in you. He, your Redeemer, is your companion. Entrust yourself to Him, and know: He is always with you, always at your side. He is the great love who is always present.

So go into the day with Christ.

February 3

Turn to Christ

Before we start any work, we should connect with Christ. The same is true for a conversation or for the solutions to various problems. We have the Inner Advisor and Helper, Christ, in us. The more often we turn to Him, asking for His will and help, the more we realize that we receive help from within.

If we then do what is lawful, that is, fulfill the commandments of God step by step, our consciousness becomes clearer, we can grasp more and more, work more purposefully and connect with our neighbor. At the same time, emotions recede, closeness emerges.

In the end, the true gain of our life lies in the day. We can discover in the day the treasures of our inner being, then, if we surrender to Christ again and again by turning to Him.

February 4

Looking good—
what does that get you?

For each of us, thoughts come already in the morning. Some of us can keep their thoughts and feelings with God; others are already drawn to the workplace, to the family, to this or that problem. Still another thinks, "How will I behave toward my colleagues in order to look good with my work, with what I say, with how I present myself?"

Let us be aware, already in the morning, that the world greets us with its impressions, opinions and ideas only briefly, and then turns back to its own problems. By "world" I mean all those people who are world-oriented, that is, ego-oriented. One thing is certain: God always looks into our heart.

February 5

Gain access to your true self

Everyone of us has *their* day because they have determined it according to their inputs in this existence on Earth or in previous incarnations. We have created it ourselves with our way of feeling, sensing, thinking, speaking and acting. Therefore, each day is the creation of each individual. We could also say: In our day our own, personal law is active.

Say yes to this new day, which is your day, and you will experience yourself in your day. You will also experience yourself in your contact with your neighbor. Your reactions to what they say, which are reflected in your thinking, in your words and also in your actions—that is what you are. So recognize your all-too-human aspects. Clear them up, and you will gain access to your inner self, to the true self.

February 6

Your shallow breathing shows the restlessness of your heart, your deep breathing, the inner stillness

Do we do our daily work with God, for God and thus, for our neighbor or against God and thus, against our neighbor? Our breathing rhythm and our thoughts tell us what is good and what is less good. A shallow breath reveals the restlessness of the heart and also brings the corresponding thoughts that build up during the day.

We people should live meaningfully and also draw the consequences from the experiences of our days; for instance, in our restlessness, in our pressing thoughts, to recognize our sinfulness, clear it up and no longer do it. That is why we also close the day in the evening, by once again reflecting on everything and bringing it into divine order.

A deep breathing shows inner stillness. It is precisely inner stillness that is crucial for new strength, which we draw in the evening and at night, so that the coming day will be a sunny day.

February 7

To want to exclude everything unpleasant and disturbing from our lives creates a pseudo-harmony and an illusory life

Our day will not be good if we endeavor to exclude everything unpleasant and disturbing from our life and strive to create and maintain a pseudo-harmony. That would be an illusory life, a house of cards that is arduous to make and maintain and which sooner or later collapses.

Your day is a good day when you live it consciously and attentively, that is, when you hear what the moment, the situation and the occurrence of the day want to tell you. Then you clarify, put in order and clear up what needs to be clarified, put in order and cleared up. Then you recognize, work on and erase the small and bigger shadows in your soul. In this way we establish a peaceful and harmonious communication with our fellow people, but also with the things that occupy us intensely, that put pressure on us.

February 8

Free yourself from pressing thoughts, then the powers of God can flow to you in prayer

The first thoughts of your day show you who you are and what you perhaps take into the day. If you allow one all-too-human thought to build on another, so that your body and disposition come into increased vibration, then you can hardly grasp a prayer thought.

If you pray anyway, it is a superficial prayer. We may think thoughts of prayer, but where are our feelings and sensations? It is a divided prayer:

The thoughts are with God, but our feelings and sensations are with our wishes and needs.
If we want to pray from the heart, if we want to fill our prayer thoughts with our sensations and feelings, that is, to raise our heart to God, we write down our pressing needs and desires in order to analyze them *after* our prayer. By writing down what urges us, we become free and can turn to God and pray deeply. Then the powers of God can flow to us.

February 9

Open a spiritual book and read! The words have a message for you

If it is possible for you, you can, if you like, open a spiritual book. Indeed, just take it and open it wherever it happens to open today, and then look inside and read the words on which your eye falls. Nothing happens by chance. The words that are written on these opened pages speak to you. They want to communicate to you. Try it out.

If you are ready to accept this advice, then go within with what you have read and compare the words with your life on Earth. If it is possible for you to do this in peace, then you will also have valuable impulses for today and possibly for further steps in your life on Earth.

February 10

Rest for your soul through the positive alignment of the consciousness

If we are drawn to a meditative prayer today, we may be responding to the call of our stressed soul.

Meditative prayer means to go within, to immerse in the depth of the very basis of our soul, to feel our prayers with our heart and to fulfill what we pray with the power of our heart, of our consciousness, as it were. If we let our prayer become reality by fulfilling what we have prayed in our life, then our day will also be fulfilled and our soul can recover from our all-too-human thinking. Then it receives the desired rest.

FEBRUARY 11

You can turn your fate around yourself

Our fate—that is what we ourselves are.
We determine our fate ourselves; we ourselves shape it in a friendly way or filled with tension. But no one is at the mercy of their fate! No one has to despair; no one has to be resigned.
We create our fate ourselves—and we ourselves can turn it around! How? Through self-recognition and clearing up with the power of our Redeemer, Christ.

FEBRUARY 12

Experience yourself in your thoughts and words

Thoughts and words are symbols that contain the reality about ourselves. In every thought, in every word, is the key that unlocks the door of our being, so that we can better recognize our nature, that is, our character.

If your work for the day leaves you some free time, think about the content of your thoughts. In this way, you take in hand the key to experiencing your character, that is, your traits.

If you like, the day ahead of you could be under the motto: Experience yourself! Ask Christ for help, so that you become a good self-explorer and the day makes you aware of what you may recognize today.

February 13

Find your way to the right deed in Christ, and become a bringer of light

The day brings us quite a few experiences. Have you been able to interpret the symbolic language of what you have already encountered today? If not, don't be annoyed or sad. Everything takes practice.

Only once we have explored ourselves, for example, by splitting open, so to speak, our own thoughts and words, in order to find and clear up their content, then with this experience in overcoming our all-too-human aspects, we can also better understand our neighbor, thus getting to know them in their words and work.

Take Christ with you into the rest of your day! Ask Him that you may become a conscious self-explorer who recognizes his mistakes, his sinfulness, clears it up and no longer does it. Then your deeds will become more selfless, because your thoughts and words are more God-conscious.

The world is calling for righteous deeds, because much has been thought and spoken about Christ, but now the world needs the convincing proof. You, too, can be a little bringer of light into this dark world!

February 14

Do you want to walk toward the light or still remain in the shadows?

Our spiritual body, the pure being in our soul, is immortal. Through Christ, our Redeemer, it enters the light again. But each of us has the freedom to walk toward the light today or to still remain in the shadows.

You decide this.

February 15

What do you want to do with your personal shadow?

The shadow in which many a person tarries is their own personal shadow. They have created it themselves. Through what? Through the law: What we sow—shadow or light—we will reap; there is where we will live.

We sow through what goes out from us: through our deeds and words, but also through our thoughts, sensations and feelings. Each of us reaps as he or she has sown, and thus, we will also experience joy and sorrow out of what we have sown. Through what we sow, we create our own law that determines our days.

What do you want to do with your personal shadow?

February 16

Gain life force and physical strength with concentration and the positive alignment of your thoughts

If you can grant your soul peace again and again through a positive alignment of your thinking, the alignment of your consciousness, then you will soon realize that you have much more life force, that is, also physical strength, than when you let go of the rudder of your ship of life by letting your thoughts constantly go here and there.

The tranquility of the soul also gives us, the person, peace and a good communication with our neighbors, because we then also understand them better. We will no longer judge so often, but will become more understanding, because the tranquility of the soul makes flow to us the divine streams of love and peace.

February 17

See what you are doing wrong, change it—and you will become happy and free

Self-recognition is the help for a better understanding of our fellow people—as long as we work on the beam in our eye, which Jesus pointed out to us in His teaching with the image of the beam and the splinter.

If we were to see only what our neighbor might be doing wrong, we would become disgruntled and reproachful, but not happy and free. To become free means to see and work on the beam in our eye. If we make use of this today, we will certainly change toward the positive in some aspects.

The blessing of God flows eternally. If we have created a riverbed for God's blessing to flow through, we will feel it.

February 18

What you have left behind you— do not do it anymore!

What you have left behind you by clearing things up—do not do it anymore. Resolve firmly how you want to deal with it in the future. Indeed, prescribe for yourself how you want to think and act. You can also write it down; this will give you a good guideline and a good basis for the coming hours and days.

If you keep it up, you will soon realize that peace enters you, and you feel joyful and strengthened. Then you will feel that you have accepted and made use of your day as a day of grace.

FEBRUARY 19

God is there.
He is in all things

If you like, take the following thoughts of dawning awareness and inwardness into yourself. They will convey to you security and nearness to God:
The Spirit of God is close to us at every moment.
He is the power in us!
Let us be aware that:
Wherever we are—God is there!
God is the positive energy in all things.
God is the life!
God is the solution of all difficulties and problems.
God is the health in every illness.
God is in all things.

Once we become more and more aware of this, we gradually tap into the inner life, our divine heritage. Doubt and despair are overcome. We sense how the inner sun permeates us.

February 20

Sincerely affirm the good in your neighbor, then you will transform many a heart

If you like, take in the following wisdom of life: "We are in this world to develop peace in ourselves and to live in peace with our fellow people." The first step toward inner peace is the sincere understanding of our fellow people—whatever they say and do. If we succeed in this, then we will also find the good in our neighbor.

Let us sincerely affirm the good in our neighbor, and let us also speak about it with appreciation! Then we will transform many a heart.

February 21

Organize your day with God and find your way into the guidance of God and His all-wise loving powers

If you wish, go into a brief but deep morning prayer at the beginning of the day. Let your soul pray, and speak out the thoughts. Let the words flow back into you, as it were. You will quickly realize that they have a calming effect on you. You suddenly become quieter, more balanced, more harmonious. Your consciousness expands. Becoming still from within also means gaining tranquility, which, in turn, leads to prudence and concentration. You need concentration for your daily work; let Christ give it to you by praying to Him from your heart.

If you feel in yourself that you want to shape your day with God, then you will find yourself guided by God and His all-wise, loving powers.

February 22

In your good resolutions lies the strength, so that some things will go better in the future

Good resolutions are positive principles in which there is the strength and confidence that some things will go better in the future, because we have decided for the good, for God.

The positive result of our self-exploration, the good guideline of how we want to do things in the future, should be written down in keywords, if possible. This can help us when the same or similar situations come toward us.

February 23

You are a part of the great Creator-power. The elements want to serve you

Each day has its mood, which is also determined by the elemental forces. We could become aware and take to heart that we, like the elemental forces, are a part of the great Creator-power and that the elements want to serve us, if we accept them as we encounter them at the moment. They speak to us when we respect and heed them, thus entering into communication with them. What might the warm ray of sunshine say to you as it shines through the window? What might the water that flows over you when you wash your body in the morning say to you? What message does the earth you walk on, the air you breathe, have for you?

Be aware: The elements want to serve humankind. How do you, the human being, behave toward the elements?

February 24

Become independent and steadfast in yourself

Several aids for becoming free of our pressing desires:
"Remember: God knows what is good for us and He wants only the best for us. If we grow into this awareness—God wants only the best for us; He is always with us, always the listener and helper in every situation—then we become quiet and attain the experience that God is guiding us."
This gives us stability; in this way we become independent and steadfast in ourselves.

FEBRUARY 25

Your good resolutions go with you through the day

Have you made some good resolutions?
The positive inputs from the morning will help you during the day. Give honor to God in everything. If you strive to feel accepted by Him, your day will be good. Surrender it to Christ. If there are still things that concern you, it is helpful to remedy them, so that the day will be in the spirit of your day's input, that is, your good resolution. A help so that we keep reminding ourselves of this during the hours of the day could be to write down our guideline, our resolution. We write the sentence, this positive statement, on a piece of paper or in a small booklet that we carry with us. Whenever the situation allows us, we take it out and read what we have written down.

February 26

Seek the causes for disagreements in yourself

The day is a fulfilling day when you can do your work in a concentrated way and according to plan, when you are in harmony with your colleagues, when communication flows among each other, when everything is in the proper order.

If the day brings incidents and agitations, do not complain about the colleague or the boss. First of all, look for the cause of the disagreement in yourself and rectify it with the power of the Christ of God in you. In this way, you will regain your inner balance and you will very soon realize that, for example, the conversations will be much more balanced.

The attempt is worth it. Try it!

February 27

"Either for or against Me"

Our thoughts are either positive or negative. There is nothing in-between. As Jesus, the Christ, said: Either for or against Me. Therefore, here, too, there is no halfway.

Those who try to recognize themselves also get to know their neighbor, the good as well as the less good sides.

I wish for you that in the evening you can say: It was the will of God that set everything that I thought, said and did into movement. I did not get my energy from my fellow people, but I received it from God, because I gave what I expected from others, for example, respect and appreciation.

February 28

The positive power, God, is also in what is unpleasant and difficult

The positive power, God, is in all situations of your day. It is also in the situations and occurrences that are unpleasant and difficult. Find it!

February 29

Every situation can change when we change something about ourselves

Just by making an effort to say "stop" to yourself in a situation, that is, to pause and find the positive in it, you gain inner distance from the difficulty. You are able to look over and see through the situations more clearly, and what could be done will perhaps occur to you.

Therefore, you should get into the habit of not immediately reacting to negative things in a human emotional way, but to take a step back and reflect on the positive, which is certainly there, too, though often still blocked by our negative feelings and thoughts.

Every situation can change. Mostly it changes when we change something—of course, in ourselves, in our thoughts and feelings.

March 1

The desire to take center stage— an actor among actors

*M*any of us think that we have to be the center of life on Earth. Everyone has to revolve around us; otherwise they would be against our opinion and therefore against us.

How many act and twist themselves—just to get a little recognition, to be the center of attention in the family, the circle of friends or among co-workers. Many people keep their mental carousel going in this regard with the recurring question: Am I or am I not the center? How do I get the attention of everyone? What should I do, how should I act, what pose should I take, in order to direct the attention to myself?

The principle is: Like attracts like. According to this principle, if we want to be the center of our existence, we should ask ourselves: How many actors, have I, the actor, attracted? How many actors do I have around me who are the same or similar as me, who applaud me, so that they also get the necessary applause, the necessary energy for their ego?

March 2

You do not live solely for yourself

Remember: You do no live solely for yourself. Life in God consists of being with and for one another. Every component of the inner life contains everything. And every creature is there for everyone and for everything.

If you become aware of this, then you will go into the day peacefully and joyfully. You will affirm and also find the good in all things. This is the help in many situations—the help also for your neighbor.

March 3

Knowing about the why makes each of your feelings invaluable

Whether we experience enjoyable or unpleasant things, both can become positive components of our lives.
Therefore, pause and review the situations of the past hours. Which experiences, which incidents, which encounters have pleased you? Again, ask "why"—why they were positive and enjoyable for you. What was good today, what you thought and did correctly today, you would certainly like to continue doing so tomorrow, and perhaps tomorrow you would like to build on what you have gained and experienced today. Even what is not good has its causes. In any case, it is good to become aware of the why and perhaps write it down in keywords in your journal.

March 4

Dissolve with Christ the clouds on the horizon of your feelings and sensations

Have you decided to achieve inner freedom, to let the sun of love and peace shine again? Make the clouds disperse by dissolving them with Christ.

Maybe you will say, "It's not that easy!"

Well, look into your thoughts and feelings. What don't you want to let go of? What have you become attached to? Bindings are created only by our sinful ego. They oppress us; they are the clouds on the horizon of feelings and sensations. You have the free choice to keep what oppresses you or to dissolve it with Christ. If you like, dissolve the unrest. If you clear up what is pending, you will become more harmonious.

MARCH 5

Become kind.
Then you will reach the One
who is good: GOD

*Y*our neighbor wants to be happy; you also want to be happy. So bring a little happiness to your neighbor, some selfless feelings, some selfless thoughts; learn to understand them, and you will begin to bring more and more happiness and receive happiness yourself. You decide for yourself whether you want to do it that way.

God is always good. Gradually develop kindness in yourself. If we become kind, we will reach the One who is good: God. And we will become honest and truthful.

March 6

Stand by your positive inputs, even when your day goes in a different way

Your day does not always go as you input in the morning. But, if you can say, "I recognized and cleared up several things and I will keep doing what was good," then in this way you affirm the positive and it will continue in a positive way.

March 7

You decide about your further path in life— by setting goals and planning

You yourself determine your coming days.
A clear goal and good planning is always a help.

March 8

Positive thoughts make possible the impossible

The positive powers want to go with you into the day. They also help you to understand your neighbor.

Those who seek to understand their fellow people become more open and straightforward, creating the conditions for a positive communication with them. Surely you have the opportunity to practice this today. In the family, among friends or relatives, we can apply what we have recognized, and then continue to practice understanding in everyday life, with our colleagues, with the boss, so that we gain more and more understanding.

Know: Positive thoughts are radiant forces. They form a great chain of lights that makes possible the impossible.

March 9

You can give your life a new direction!

In the morning—and if possible also during the day—allow yourself time for rest and reflection. Take a look into the book of your present life, into your feelings and sensations. They are the soil from which your thoughts grow. What is moving in you?

Perhaps you feel the stillness of the morning, the freshness of the air, the awakening in nature. You may also have memories of what you were able to positively overcome yesterday. Or you feel glad, for example, about a good, clarifying conversation. But surely other things are stirring as well. Discord with a fellow person or even illness and worry because some external things are not as you expect and want them to be?

You can give your life a new direction. How?— Give what you expect!

March 10

Your morning prayer thoughts are your guide and companion through the day

If you have lifted your heart to God in the morning, then you know your prayer thoughts. Become aware of them and take them with you into the day. They are your guide and companion, because we want to fulfill our prayers. It is not by chance that you sent certain prayer thoughts to God. Heed the following: What they contain is of special importance for your day today.

You are not merely encountering people, things, and situations today. May I tell you that you will also encounter your thoughts and your feelings? What you see calls up feelings and thoughts in you. These are signs of the day for you. How do you relate to these? Apply your morning prayer, and you will experience the help. Therefore, if you wish, use your morning prayer as a guide through the day.

March 11

The energy of the day brings many opportunities to change some things to the positive

The energy of the day makes you aware of many things. It shows you some things that you can now do better.

The energy of the day, the moment of the day, also makes you aware of yourself, of your mistakes, when your colleague is unpleasant to you or when your boss has touched a correspondence by pointing out things that do not correspond to the rules of procedure. Especially when you are upset or angry, you clearly feel that something is moving inside you: your weakness, your wrong attitude, your guilt—not that of your fellow people. Thus, your day brings you many opportunities to change toward the positive.

March 12

In the affirmation of the inner values lies the key for a conscious life

Jesus taught us to become images of the eternal Father. In this, His teachings, lies the hope and the fact that this can be and will be.

However, if we keep thinking about our weakness and baseness and identify ourselves with this and with the sinner that we surely are, then things will not get better with us. We will reinforce what we mentally presume to be, that is, attribute it to ourselves, as it were.

Thoughts are forces with which we work and which bring about what we give to them. Through our thoughts we can condemn ourselves to be weak or a sinner, as it were, and to remain so.

However, if we change our thinking, if we think and speak of the inner strength, the inner wealth, which also becomes effective externally when we gradually fulfill the commandments of God, or that we are indeed sinners, but that we will clear up our recognized sins with the help of the Christ of God, our Redeemer, and no longer do them, then we have a good basis for our further life. Our view widens, hope and confidence return—and things will get better.

March 13

Each of your neighbors has positive traits. They are also in you. Affirm them!

It is up to us, to each one of us, what we make of our life, of our day.

Remember: The path to God is simple. It goes by way of our neighbor. The truth is also simple. If you remain faithful to the truth, your life will also go well, because then God, the Great One, can arrange everything for you. God is not complicated—God is ingenious, and the ingenious is always the simple.

Become calm and relaxed. Reflect on the good. Realize that each of your neighbors has positive qualities. They are also in you! Affirm them!

March 14

Prepare yourself for the new day. Move in God's law and love

Surely you will be dealing with people today. Remember that they can also be mirrors for you. What irritates you about them is an irritant in your soul. Find it and overcome it!

Prepare yourself for the new day! Move in God's law and love. Then there will be no standstill in your life, no rigidity. You won't get rusty, so to speak. We do not become rusty and frosty—we become joyful and a conscious overcomer of our all-too-human aspects, our base, egotistical, petty self.

In this awareness, begin the new day! Christ is with you.

March 15

A good plan in God's hand is a good co-worker

The outer and inner plan for the day can be a great help. It helps you to look forward to the day joyfully.

Include in your plan also how you will manage your tasks, how you will have positive conversations with your neighbor and how you will fulfill your tasks to satisfaction. In this way, you prepare for the coming day and already input positive energies, especially when you place this plan in the hands and will of our heavenly Father.

A good plan in God's hands is a good co-worker.

March 16

The content of your world makes you unhappy or happy

The individual's personal world is made up of the content of their days, weeks and years. The content of the feelings, sensations, thoughts, words and actions are different with each person. We make comparisons again and again and think that we are the same as this or that person in a certain respect. But even when we speak the same words, each of us puts aspects of *our* world into our words.

Our conscience reacts to the content of our thoughts and feelings. Our content makes us either unhappy or happy.

March 17

Give your day and your whole life a new, positive direction

Each day brings to each one of us our own part, because it reflects back to us a part of our unresolved past. But the mirrors from the past need not frighten us, because Christ is here, the light, the power in us.

If we start the new day with Christ, we can give our day, and our whole life, a new, positive direction. The many human thoughts that intensely move us early in the morning can decisively shape our day if we do not look at them with Christ early in the morning and clear them up with His help, and then go into deep prayer.

Pray from the heart, and firmly resolve to fulfill your prayers.

March 18

There is so much power in trustful thanksgiving! Have courage!

As Christians, we should form the habit of giving thanks for everything, for the good and also for the less good. Especially in genuine heartfelt thanks—it is the trustful thanksgiving—there is so much strength and courage to master everything that the further days will bring.

The divine current is the omnipresent power. Experience it in the prayer of thanksgiving. Strengthen yourself through prayer. Christ helps each one of us—in the morning, in the afternoon, even in the evening. He wants to make us happy.

March 19

Swim against the current and reach the source

Perhaps you are thinking about the coming day and wondering what it will bring?
Why send ahead thoughts or even worries? Put yourself in God's hands and accept the days as they come. Only *your* days, *your* hours, *your* minutes will come to you—that is, what you have input.
As long as you swim with this stream of your thoughts, in which all your negativity vibrates, you will not stop to look at yourself, but will always say, "The others are to blame for everything." In this way, you let yourself drift with the current of the ego.

However, those who swim *against* this negative current, who accept the day, recognize themselves in the day and clear up their sinfulness may have a more difficult time than those who swim *with* the current, who simply let themselves drift and go. But those who swim against the current will recognize and clear up in time what is coming toward them: what they have already put into the stream in previous existences and in this life. This means to work on oneself, to overcome oneself with Christ. Only in this way, will each of us reach the source of life. Only in this way, will we attain the freedom and happiness we long for.

March 20

By affirming the good, the Inner Light, you find the sovereign serenity in God

"Clouds" move in every now and then for every person. The view becomes duller, the disposition is overshadowed. But it depends on how long we nurture the clouds. If we meet them by affirming that God, the great almighty sun, shines in us, that God's love, wisdom and greatness wants to help and support us, then with the help of the Christ of God, with the Inner Light, with this inner sun, we will dissolve the clouds so that the sunny disposition, the sovereign serenity in God, can break through again.

We should clear up existing unpleasantness, either immediately or later, through the power of thoughts or with a phone call, through a unifying letter or with an appropriate conversation.

We wish you a good day, the light of the inner sun, a serene disposition, a conciliatory and understanding look and a heart that beats in affirmation for the good, for the Inner Light, for the inner warmth, for the sovereign serenity!

March 21

Your inner gladness, the warmth of your heart, awakens strength and confidence in your neighbor

We are all on the path to constant inner happiness, to constant inner peace.

An old saying goes, "If you want to be happy in life, contribute to the happiness of others; for the joy we give returns to our own hearts."

By clarifying the various situations that we encounter, we very gradually become joyful from within. Inner joy is also inner happiness, so that we also please our neighbor with our happiness

and possibly make him a gift through a balanced and cheerful conversation.
Just your balanced cheerfulness can contribute to a good togetherness. What falls into the heart of our neighbor also touches the soul of our neighbor and brings strength and confidence to our fellow people. The inner balance, the warmth of the heart, the inner happiness, radiates to our neighbors, to our fellow people, and touches them in soul and heart.

March 22

Use the possibilities of the day; increase the light; gain joy and togetherness

God, your eternal Father, has placed you in the new day because this day, which is also your day, has a lot in store for you. What does it hold in store? For example, many opportunities for self-recognition, but also joy and togetherness.

With honest self-recognition, we lift a veil from ourselves, so to speak, and see ourselves as we really are as human beings. If we clear up our shadows, then the light increases and with it the joy and thankfulness toward God. We then experience more and more community with our neighbor, because we also see a lot of positive things in them and because our inner joy radiates, because it infects our neighbors, as it were, with cheerfulness.

March 23

Go with the help of the Christ of God onto your own test bench

If you want to get to know yourself, if you want to put yourself to the test to find out whether your thinking and speaking serve toward your perfection, then go into prayer with this and ask Christ for help and support for this day, indeed, for all the days of your life, because each day brings different thoughts. Each day stimulates us to say this or that. Thus, there are other learning steps for us in each day.

Let us examine ourselves, and we will recognize ourselves.

March 24

Does the content of your thoughts and words serve to perfect you?

We people think, think, think—without monitoring what we think. Some people talk, talk, talk—without thinking about what they are saying. This wastes a lot of energy, so that already in the morning some people are tired and listless. Let us examine ourselves in the question: How much of what we think and speak, of what occupies us during the day, serve to perfect us?

If we look at the world, we see that most people do not stand up to this test.

But we should not look at our neighbors. Let us watch ourselves in order to recognize ourselves. Let us ask again and again: Why am I thinking this way? Why am I expressing these thoughts? What are the contents of my thoughts and words? Do they serve to perfect me? Do they make me satisfied and happy? Do I find peace with them? Do I bring peace with this into this world, also into my family, into my circle of friends, into my workplace? If you like, go into your day with these questions!

March 25

"Hello, I don't want to stay this way!" The positive addresses you out of your negativity

What moves and upsets you stands before you, as it were, and calls out, "Hello! I don't want to stay this way. Hello! I don't want to be like this. Hello, can you look at me more closely, in order to cleanse me, so that I can create peace in you?" What addresses you out of your negativity is the positive—it calls you. If you have taken steps into the law of God, then you will be glad of the call. In a few minutes you can do many things with yourself. You have the strength for this.

Then your nerves will relax; your thoughts will change from peaceableness to peace, and you will go into the day with joy and confidence.

MARCH 26

You gain light and strength by monitoring and clearing up the content of your thoughts

Do not be resigned—the goodness and mercy of God helps us to overcome the most difficult and melancholy thoughts and feelings. The mercy and goodness of the Almighty helps us to analyze our words in the question: Why did I have to say this or that? What did I want to achieve with it? And: What did it bring me?

Clear up the content of your thoughts and words with Christ, and firmly resolve not to entertain and utter these thoughts or words again. In time, you will succeed better and better, because these thoughts and words will soon lose their power. And you will become more alert, more secure, more conscious; you will save yourself a lot of time and will gain more and more recognition and insights. In this way, you gain in light and strength.

March 27

Wanting to look good before others— is it worth the effort?

A common fault is that we want to look good before our fellow people.

Have we ever asked ourselves: What good does it do for us if we do everything we can to look good in front of people? Will it make us more satisfied and free? Maybe for a few moments, when we receive encouragement, confirmation and appreciation from our fellow people. But how long does the effect of this energy of encouragement, the energy of appreciation last? Then we are again dissatisfied, unhappy or even depressed. Is it worth the effort?

March 28

People are discontent as long as they sin

People will be discontent as long as they sin. If they gradually clear up their sinfulness, they will become more peaceful, and their dealings with their neighbors will be benevolent and selfless.

March 29

What flows from the heart goes into the heart of your neighbor

If today you are occasionally alone with your thoughts, then you have the opportunity to recognize yourself more and more deeply. If you come together with your fellow people, who are your brothers and sisters, then remember: Learn to understand your neighbor, then you will also make yourself more understandable for your fellow people, your brothers and sisters. For what flows from the heart goes into the heart of your neighbor.

Perhaps you would like to remind yourself of this wisdom more often today. Try it. If you practice it, you will gradually succeed more and more, and it will make you happy.

March 30

Apply what you have recognized. In this way, you reach unity with yourself

As often as possible, we should apply what we have recognized as truth; we should practice it. Then we will gain certainty in it. How are you doing with this? Many of us fulfill these principles again and again, and were privileged to experience that we then become one with ourselves and also with our neighbor.

To come into unity with ourselves and also with our neighbor means to connect with God. This fills the heart and makes us happy.

Those who give, receive. If you keep this up today, then you will experience: Give from the heart, and you will receive from the heart. This sustains us and leads us to the inner communication with Christ, our Brother and Redeemer.

March 31

Through your positive thinking and behavior, ask for the higher values of life

Those who affirm the good and want the best for their neighbor and ask for the divine laws, the higher values of life, in everything that the day brings will find them.

April 1

Recognize, decide, discard and act; then you are free

If you like, take a little reminder with you into your day:
When your thoughts wrap around you,
you are trapped.
Recognize, decide, discard and *be*—
act accordingly, and you are free.

April 2

The optimist works out what is good and stays with it

How do we do our day's work? Do we stay true to ourselves and follow our good intentions, or do we let ourselves go and fall into our old, dreary thought patterns, which always have a trace of reproach? Are we just to ourselves and become just to our fellow people? Thus, are we an optimist who works out the good in everything and adheres to the good? Or are we a pessimist who contributes to the veiling and darkening of many a matter?

Always restore balance in yourself as soon as possible. This is the best prerequisite for a positive day and in the evening, for a good and restful sleep, resulting in a bright and shining face and the corresponding positive, confident, affirmative thoughts.

April 3

Recognize in the sending potential what you will receive

The law of God is love. In order to attain the law of God, the love, we should become aware that everything that is against love is unloving.
We should get rid of what is unloving—on the path of clearing up everything that moves us, that brings our correspondence, our disposition, into turmoil.
It is an immutable law: we will receive what we send. The effect is already contained in the sending potential. God-filled thoughts are thoughts of love that unite and link. Egoistic thoughts are unloving thoughts that separate and conjure up what we put into them. They show the fateful features of our human existence.
What do you want to send?

April 4

Open up the present in you— listen to what the voice of your day says to you

In the first thoughts of the day we hear, as it were, the voice of our day. In the moments, in the situations of our day, our own inputs speak, our energy potentials, which we have entered during this earthly existence or previous existences by means of our feeling, thinking, speaking and acting.

Since no thought, no feeling and no word is lost, these energies are stored in the atmosphere, in our soul and also in the respective heavenly bodies that take in our inputs. They come back to us by way of our world of thoughts or in the situations of our day.

If we make use of our day, if we listen to the voice of the day, if we hear our inputs, so that we then clear them up with the help of the Christ of God, we no longer build on our future, but we create the present in us; because by clearing up our sinfulness—which we then also no longer do—we open up our divine heritage and thus, the direct way to the Father's house. This is then the opening of our eternal present—the life in God.

April 5

Gain inner peace, in order to grasp life in its depth

If you live the hours of the day consciously, you will recognize that the day richly gives to you, even if negative or grave things approach you or if even big problems come up for you. The light of the day, which is God, wants to master the situations with you, so that the inner turmoil may subside and you become more quiet in thought. In the evening, analyze the situations of the day with your conscious mind. Record what was good, that is, where you were self-possessed, and when you became unsettled. Look again at what followed from this and how you mastered it or did not yet master it. If, as soon as possible and with the power of the Christ of God, you resolve what still makes you uneasy, then you will experience more and more the stillness of thought, which enables you to grasp life in its depth and to fulfill God's will.

April 6

By clearing up what we recognize, an aspect of strength can develop

Often already in the early morning our thoughts revolve around our neighbors, around our colleagues at work, around our boss, around our wife, husband, children, relatives or friends and acquaintances. One or the other has said or done something that touched us disagreeably and triggered a flood of thoughts in us that we couldn't restrain and that got up with us again this morning.

Often these expressions were merely opinions, sometimes merely awkwardly chosen words that got us into turmoil. By clearing up what we recognize in ourselves with this, an aspect of strength can rise from our upheaval and build up and expand.

April 7

Today is today—the present. Therein is the chance for a turnaround

You have avoided solving a problem and now think you have "done it."

This is ultimately a mistake, because the same and similar things come again. So a new day can again be the old day, possibly with suffering, pain, with the fateful traits that we could have cleared up long ago. Now the day strikes, and we are ultimately the beaten ones.

If we do not follow the impulse of our day, we make ourselves the "whipping boy." The blows will then come; but it is always we who are to blame.

When fate beats us—we ourselves have created the beating by violating the law, and now we experience the pain. But today is today, that is, the present, and therein is the chance to turn things around. Today you have the chance to explore what is not good, your uneasy feeling, to analyze it, as it were. Clear up the aspects that you become aware of and no longer do what was not good. After clearing things up, resolve for the laws of life; immerse these guidelines in your conscious mind, so that they become more and more familiar to you and you then fulfill them daily.

April 8

Going from the head to the heart. Prayer from the depths of your soul is a conversation with God

If you want to go from the head to the heart, then join us:

We breathe more deeply; we consciously breathe more deeply. Thereby our body straightens up. We continue breathing calmly and deeply. We feel how calm we become. The pressing thoughts recede, our eyes become clearer, the view widens; our breathing automatically becomes calm and deep.

Our earnest resolve to go from the head to the heart already accomplishes many things. We notice that something is drawing us in. It is a feeling of warmth, of security, of tranquility, something that cannot be described, but is there. There are fine streams from the Kingdom of God in us.

If we let these fine streams flow into our heart and mind, then we suddenly feel that we want to express this fine feeling, the resonance of inner joy and thankfulness. If you feel this, then you should pray.

This prayer is your prayer. It comes from the depths of your soul. It is a conversation with God. After the prayer, you sense that the external thoughts that may have previously determined your morning have receded; they are no longer urging and binding. Accept them, and place them in the hand of God.
If you have also placed your day in the hand of God, let the day now come to you.

April 9

The scale of feelings, your conscience, tells you what is positive and what is negative

How can we find out what is positive and what is negative?

If our level of feelings is active, then we can use it as a scale, so to speak, by weighing on the scale of feelings what the day brings or has brought us. Our feelings then signal to us whether what passes into our past is positive or negative.

For example, one day there were several conversations, perhaps problems or difficulties. Have you recognized your part? Ask your level of feelings, and at the same time you are asking your conscience. In the uneasiness in the pit of your stomach or in the rhythm of your body and, for example, your breathing, you can then read what was good and what was less good, and you can clear it up in good time.

April 10

Practice becoming still; you gather strength

If you want, practice becoming still, for from this you will truly gain spiritually.

Becoming still means briefly making an effort not to allow any thought or feeling—even if initially it is only for half a minute.

If we practice becoming still every day, and when possible during the day, it will soon become a necessity for us, because we notice that we gather a lot of strength in just a few minutes, which will help us, for example, to cope with our daily workload.

April 11

React calmly, reflect about yourself, think before you speak

We have become still in our inner being when we have discarded our urging will. But we could also practice becoming still. If by becoming still we attain stillness, we will gradually attain mastery over ourselves. Then we will also become more reflective, from which prudence emerges.

Prudent people will not immediately spout out their thoughts in words, but will first consider whether what they are thinking is of any importance, and what good it does to think that way, or even to express the thoughts. Those who first consider what they want to say and whether it is useful and to whom will more and more often think about themselves, reflecting about themselves, and thereby react more and more prudently.

April 12

Don't cling to the old, negative things; let the positive have a chance

We often think things to ourselves that we do not want. For example, if we keep thinking that we are weak, we will most likely remain weak or become even weaker, both mentally and physically. As a result of this mental behavior, we also fail to master our tasks in the school of Earth. If we keep thinking that we are sinners—then we continue to sin, because the words "we are all sinners" are, as it were, an excuse for our continual sinning. If we dwell too long on the thought "I am a sinner," we do not allow, as it were, the redemptive power of the Christ of God to take effect. We cling to our sinfulness and adhere to it as long as we do not let the positive have a chance instead, by affirming it and prescribing it to us.

April 13

Becoming still leads you into communication with the Inner Helper and Advisor, God

Take yourself back and become still. In becoming still, we practice reaching the present, which is God. By becoming still or even being still, we attain communication with the great Helper and Advisor, GOD. Then in our world of feelings, we sense more and more clearly what is cleared up, that is, past, and what is still not cleared up, the burdening, which the day would like to take into the past, into the realm of shadows.

The uneasy feelings signal to us what we should still clear up, so that it does not merge into the past as a shadow and become a future situation for us. Once we have rectified what was there, we become quieter. If we then again take up the exercise of becoming still, we may be able to experience for a few moments the difference between becoming still and being still.

April 14

Build up positive power!

Our day is again a gift from the hand of our heavenly Father, who wants the best for us. If we build on our morning thoughts, then our day will proceed in a similar way. If, for example, we awaken with thankfulness in our hearts, we will let this positive force flow into our daily work and into the encounters of the day.

Often, anger or worries from the previous day oppress us first thing in the morning. Then this means: Become active to set a new course. If we hand over unpleasant and adverse thoughts to Christ in us and clear up what is waiting to be cleared up in our thoughts, then the picture of the day will change. If we decide to leave the bad things in God and no longer nurture them in our thoughts, then we build up positive strength, which allows the rays of the eternal sun, God, to break through into our day.

April 15

Your thought, that is what you are!

*W*ho are you this morning? You will say: What a question—it's *me*, of course!

Who is the me? The me is what we think. Our thoughts are ourselves, because we think, and no one else thinks for us. Therefore, what we think is decisive. It reveals who we are.

Let's try to grasp the thoughts we had when we woke up. What moved us in our thoughts? Don't we often suppress them with excuses because they are unpleasant or uncomfortable for us? Let's look at ourselves in the mirror, because our reflection is more honest!

A good day always begins with a good resolution, which does not remain a resolution, but which we also keep. What do we resolve to change in ourselves so that we not only appear helpful, confident and peaceful, but become and are so?

April 16

Place your worries on the inner altar

An exercise for all of us: Especially when heavy thoughts have already distressed you in the morning, it is advisable to pray first. In prayer, place your worries again and again on the inner altar of God. Imagine in pictures this surrender of your worries, which you place on the altar of God. Place them again and again on the altar, where the light of the Christ of God is shining, and do this again and again in pictures. After you have done this a few times, you will notice that you have now also included yourself in this picture. You grow calmer. Your nagging thoughts move away from you. Trust in God builds up in you and from this, the security, the awareness that you have handed over the negativity to God, the kind One, who wants only the best for you.

Your prayer has brought you relief. Now thank God, our eternal Father, and Christ, our Redeemer.

Do not ask now where the nagging thoughts came from. Go into your day calm and hopeful. During the course of the day, individual ones of these nagging thoughts may reappear. Do not be angered by their appearance. Accept them! They may have a message for you, which is: You were so upset about this. The message is the "that's why" from the "why" that you unconsciously placed on the inner altar in God's hands. This means: You now recognize what has not been in order with you in this regard. And you know that this base aspect is already fading away, since you handed it over to the transforming power of God, to the light of the Christ of God.

Only the one who masters his negative aspects with Christ becomes a conqueror of his negative aspects.

April 17

Affirm the presence of God, and more cheerfulness will come into your life

Do not allow feelings of inadequacy, displeasure and worry to cloud your consciousness! If you look through these clouds and affirm the light of God, affirm His greatness and love, affirm His presence and help, affirm that He loves you, me—all of us—then it becomes brighter in you. The bank of clouds fades away. Your mood brightens. Those who practice the affirmation of God's presence will soon find that more and more cheerfulness enters their life. And those who make it a concern of theirs to affirm God, the light, the warmth, the sun, again and again during the day will in time become hopeful. Their disposition brightens more and more and they attain the confident cheerfulness that comes from within, from God's love, from the All-sun.

April 18

If you influence your fellow people, then you are co-responsible for their reactions

Consciously or unconsciously, we know that opinions are usually infiltrations of other people's ideas, which can lead to errors and a wrong way of looking at things.

If this upsets you, then perhaps ask yourself whether you haven't tried here and there to force your opinion on a neighbor or have persuaded certain people during conflicts to accept your opinion.

An opinion can be untrue or true, but it can trigger in others a flood of prejudices against third parties. Opinions we hear about others are better left unsaid. This could possibly cause emotional or physical harm to our neighbor if he or she gets upset about it and acts accordingly. You are responsible for what you cause!

April 19

Freedom means to bear responsibility for what we think, say and do

Early in the morning, our thoughts already mark our face and posture. Look at yourself in the mirror. It shows you what you are thinking, because we are the image of our thinking. In the morning, we usually have not yet put on an embellishing mask that is supposed to convey a certain image of us to our fellow people. We see more clearly.

Everyone sees themselves in the mirror as who they are. Let us ask ourselves: Do we want to stay like this? Each of us will now remain the way we want to be. Freedom means bearing responsibility for what we think, say and do. That is why no one should dictate to another.

April 20

Do you want to make use of this day in this your life or let it go by?

Do you want to create the possibility for your soul to move a little further into the light this coming night? You can achieve this by using this day and settling many a thing with Christ. Or will you shorten the path of the soul again with your binding, sinful thoughts? Do you want to give your soul impulses to enter the kingdom of light—or to become earthbound?

Know that the energy this day brings for you is for today—whether you use it or not. Energy is not lost. What stays unused will come back again someday to make us aware of our chance once more—or to intervene in our lives.

So how do you want to do it?

April 21

Every useless word is wasted energy

Whoever thinks a lot of all-too-human things or utters a lot of empty phrases loses both mental and physical strength, because every useless word is wasted energy.

During the day it would be good to check oneself often with the question: Did I understand myself? Do I actually know what I mean when I say this or that to my neighbor? What meaning, that is, what active energy, am I sending to my neighbor with my words? We can ask ourselves more questions: Am I really listening to my work colleagues during a conversation or do I make up my own rhyme of thoughts while the person next to me is talking?

Self-recognition has a positive effect when we remedy what unpleasantly vibrates in us. If it is not possible at the moment to remedy the matter that moves us, then we should entrust it to Christ in prayer.

God, the omnipresent light, the language of the heart, is the innermost part of your soul. It speaks constantly to each one of us; however, we mostly do not hear it because the noise level of our ego is far too great.

April 22

Someone who does the right thing with Christ has joy

Each one of us has the free will to do something or not to do it.

But those who do what is right with Christ have joy. Those who act against Christ ultimately create suffering for themselves, because their thoughts carry with them as a consequence what the individual puts into his world of thoughts.

April 23

Do not be the slave of your negative thoughts and worries

One often hears the saying: As the morning, so the evening. But is this really so? Do we have to let the serious, worrying thoughts that might have assailed us in the morning determine the course of our day? We don't have to! Rather, we should be able to say at the end of the day: As I have determined the morning, so it has carried me into the day. Or: As I have behaved during the day, so is my evening.

Perhaps you will experience today that we do not have to be the slave of our negative thoughts and our worries, if we trustingly turn to God, our Father, if we place what burdens us on the inner altar, where the light of the Christ of God is burning, which makes us free.

April 24

God wants to walk with you through your life on Earth

Wherever we go—God is always with us. Whatever we think, speak and do—God hears us. God hears us; God sees us; God lives in us. He wants to walk with us through this existence on Earth. Let us give Him the chance by aligning ourselves with God and with Christ, our Redeemer, and our life will become more and more meaningful.

April 25

Every serious effort is rewarded

In your journal, there may be the guiding principle that you have given yourself, which reads, for example, "I look for and find the positive in every situation and in every person." How are you doing with this?

Whether you have succeeded many times or only a few is of secondary importance. The active effort, the pausing in the situation in an effort to find the positive, the good—that is what counts. And every serious effort is rewarded. You then feel the subtle joy and contentment in your inner being. That is God, who is the good. In this joy, He brings His answer to you in your world of feelings and sensations. In this joy, there is also the courage and the momentum to keep on practicing this small task.

April 26

New, positive perspectives for your life emerge from the message of your day

The new day is given to you as a gift, because it has a lot ready for you. You ask: What does it bring me? If we watch ourselves every day, if we register what we see, hear, smell, taste and touch and what our reactions are, then we will gradually sense what the day wants to tell us.

The message of the day to us is nothing foreign to us. What we have entered during past earthly days as feelings, sensations, thoughts, words and actions as energy into the atmospheric memory, also into the heavenly bodies and into our soul returns to us step by step. New positive perspectives for our life emerge from the recognition and by clearing up our wrong attitudes.

April 27

You are not alone; Christ helps. Affirm the good in the movements of your day

You are not alone.

Each of us knows that life brings movement. This movement is good if we affirm the good in our negative aspects, in our surge of emotions, and clear up what is not good with the help of the Christ of God. Then our cross will be lighter and we will attain the resurrection in Christ through His cross.

Clearing things up brings calmness.

Remember: Christ wants to make you happy.

April 28

What upsets you is not your neighbor's fault, but your own—your correspondence

Do you want to apprehend the language of the day? Your day speaks into *your* thoughts and into your disposition. It does not knock on your door only from within, but also from the outside through the words or actions of *our* neighbor. How do *we* react? What do we feel and what do we think?

That is *our* part. What is in us comes into motion. For example, we feel anger, rage, rejection, rebellion; but what we feel is not the fault of our fellow person. It is the correspondence in us—our own fault. What upsets us is the part we need to look at more closely and clear up.

April 29

A brief immersion into life brings you strength and dynamism for the daily performance of duties

The daily conscious performance of one's duties is growing in the Spirit of God. From this also results the desire for immersion through meditation. Christian meditation means to immerse oneself in the great All-life, God.

What is needed is not hours of meditation, but a brief immersion in the life and in situations. If we do this again and again, it brings us strength and the dynamism to fulfill our daily duties.

April 30

> Release yourself from the pressure of your past. The courage to tackle this grants you strength and a calm, confident heart.

Each day brings us aspects from the past—shadows from former days on Earth or blows of fate. What do we do with them? Will we let what we once burdened ourselves with and what came into our awareness again today, be taken into the past by the day yet again, possibly reinforced by our thinking? Then we can be sure that we will meet these shadows again in future afflictions.

If we clear up the impulses from the day, what upsets us, what hits us, that is, what corresponds to us, our correspondences, then we gradually release ourselves from the pressure of the past. What has been cleared up and what we no longer do is past; the shadows are dissolved. The day will then be filled with more light, we become more free and draw nearer to God, which means: We live in the present more and more. Then we also become more still and already in the morning, can sense aspects of the day. We are no longer "day-blind" and no longer feel powerless, at the mercy of an unknown fate. Already in the morning we take our day actively into our hands. We take a determined look at what is not good that shows up in our feelings and thoughts, in order to recognize and clear up what we have caused.

The courage to tackle things and the decisiveness that it will be different in the future gives us strength and a joyful, confident heart.

May 1

We experience ourselves in deep prayer

Should you feel the need for self-reflection during the day, then a small piece of advice—of course, if you want.
Go briefly into prayer. Surely you can find a quiet place, or walk a few steps to where there are few people, and pray. It is in deep prayer, in the prayer of faith, that we experience ourselves and relive our pros and cons, so that we can consciously take the further steps on our path through life.

May 2

Find your way into your center, where God is, the power and the life

God is in everyone and everything.
He is omnipresent. He is present in each leaf that falls from a tree, in the ray of sun that breaks through the cloud cover and touches you, in the wind that plays around your face and ruffles your hair. You hear the beating of raindrops on the window—it is God. Become aware of this!

Practice finding God in all things. And if it is only the small, bright flash in the awareness that says: "Yes, He is here!" These are the first steps, in order to find our way more and more into the center—into our own center, where God is.

For the center in all things is the power and the life, God.

May 3

Make the best of your day!

Make the best of the situations, the incidents, the moments of your day! Now and then bring to mind the statement "God is always there for me," then God, the positive power in all things, also in your thinking, speaking and doing, can become effective. Many a difficult situation can also be mitigated or even resolved when we turn to God.

May 4

You can change yourself

Good morning, dear brother, dear sister.
God has again placed you in this new day. On this day, too, He wants to say many things to you. He speaks through countless mouths. He speaks through your family members as well as through your colleagues. He speaks through your five senses and in your reactions shows you who you still are.

The little word "still" means: As you are in this moment, you don't need to be in the next moment. You can change. Thus, we could ask ourselves, what should we change this day so that we can say in the evening that we have truly lived?

May 5

Today you have the strength to remedy what you recognized today

If you discover unpleasant things in your world of feelings and thoughts, such as envy, being self-opinionated and arrogant, know this: If we recognize that these sinful aspects are our own and want to clear them up, we also have the strength to remedy them.

If we clear up our sinful aspects and no longer do them, the light in our soul becomes stronger. At the same time, however, the shadows that still exist come into movement. And that is good, because they show us what still wants to be overcome.

May 6

God, the light and the strength, is always present

God, the light and the strength, is always present. God is in all Being, also in every component of matter. God, the light, the power, is in every word that you speak. He is in every thought, every feeling, every stirring. God is also in all that you do, because God is the Being, the all-permeating life, which sustains the nature kingdoms, each soul and each human being.

God is our eternal Father; we are His children. To prove yourself as a child of God means to fulfill His commandments.

Each day is a part of our life. In each aspect of this part of the day, we find God and ourselves. Everything sinful is more easily resolved when we are aware of the power in everything that is our life.

May 7

Pray from the heart. Accompany your thoughts with your feelings and sensations

If you have time to think about yourself more, if you have time to pray more deeply and longer, then withdraw for a short time. If you wish, go into a short prayer meditation. This means:

Do not search for words in your conscious mind. Sit quietly, and let the prayer thoughts rise up from deep within you. Accompany your thoughts with your feelings and sensations. Pause again and again, so that your thoughts can also form images.

Thus, pray from the heart. Then you are in unity with your thoughts and with your inner being and will find your way into the stillness more and more.

May 8

Stand consciously in the day. Face whatever comes toward you

The new day begins.
What do you want to make of it? Do you want to let yourself be determined by the hours, the moments of the day and by what they bring you? Or do you want to consciously stand in the day and face what comes to you with the moment? You decide for yourself.

If you are alert, then you live *with* the day. Whatever it reflects to you—recognize yourself in it and clear it up. Then give yourself a new, positive guiding thought, a principle from God's law. And then act in the same way.

May 9

Christ is the life force in you and the courage to face life

We live on this Earth so that we recognize ourselves. But we want to outgrow this school on Earth, the daily effort of recognizing and clearing up our mistakes and weaknesses! If these are worked off, erased with the help of the Christ of God, then we have completed the Earth school; we live in the law of God and are taken into God's love and wisdom.

Do not become resigned, dear brother, dear sister. Each new day is given to us so that we look at ourselves anew and again see ourselves in a new garment of life force and the courage to face life, for Christ is the life force and the courage to face life in us.

May 10

Divine will and wisdom lead into a creative life

Our Father, who created us, the great love and wisdom, is the "let there be," from which the deed is fulfilled. He, the great Spirit, is always active according to His divine will, for will and wisdom reach out to one another. It is the creative forces that bring forth spiritually manifested life.

Thus, we are also called upon not to be idle. We should use our mind, which we have received as human beings. A healthy human understanding that weighs without prejudice is a good scale that collects divine knowledge and thus communicates to the person. If we act according to our inner insights that have been weighed, then we will increasingly find our way into a creative life that fulfills us and serves our fellow people.

May 11

What we sow is in our hands

We should nurture positive thoughts: thoughts of love for our neighbor, thoughts of friendship, of hope, confidence, thoughts that God is with us. The positive seed also has its time to mature. It brings us peace, happiness and a life fulfilled from within.

What do we plant today in the field of our soul—a good or less good seed?
What we sow is in our hands.

May 12

Do not fail! Christ is the power that sets you free

Dear brother, dear sister, do not fail! What is not yet in order in you now shows itself through the energy of the day. It wants to be remedied. It is important not to seek the blame with your fellow people, with the boss, with a colleague or with others. That would not help you any further. Look for the cause in yourself. Ask yourself: What was in you that made you react like that?

What irritates us about our fellow people—that is what we are ourselves. So have courage to look at yourself honestly. That is the first big step. Then be glad about your self-recognition. Repent, in your heart ask for forgiveness from your neighbor, forgive. And resolve to be good and to act with understanding for your fellow people in the future. Do it with Christ. He is the power that sets you free.

May 13

Give yourself a positive image of your day in the spirit of the Sermon on the Mount

After a heartfelt morning prayer, you can create a positive image of your day by specifying how you want to meet your fellow people, how you want to tackle your work, and possibly that you want to fulfill it with the power of the Christ of God ...

If you then do what you have set out to do, that is, if you put your plan into practice in the spirit of the Ten Commandments of God and of the Sermon on the Mount of Jesus, you will soon realize how near to you the helping, loving power is, God, and will notice that your day is balanced and harmonious.

Should difficulties and problems come up, then your positive attitude will help you to resolve this situation with the help of the Lord. Then your day will be a good day.

May 14

Prudent speaking is a help for self-recognition

Those who think about what they say remain focused. Those who talk a lot are distracted. They are not aware of their mostly disordered activity of thought, thus losing a lot of energy.

If you take these indications into your day, you will realize that many a thought, many a situation wants to compel you to talk. Why? Ask yourself: Do you, the person, want to communicate or display yourself—or do you want to clarify the situation with the help of the Inner Light? Then you will also speak prudently and not use too many words about the matter.

If you like, you can take these aids with you into the day. They are like a seismograph that always points out what we are lacking.

May 15

The day points out your inputs

We once had contact with someone, and have almost forgotten them—and now this person passes us on the sidewalk among many other people. We feel affected. Thoughts, feelings come up—in the pictures of our memory we see, as it were, a secret from our past.

We see ourselves in the picture and see our fellow person. We feel how we thought about him. We have pangs of conscience: Back then, when we had contact with this person we thought and spoke badly about him. We disparaged him, judged him. He doesn't know this; it was our secret.

Now we have become aware of it. The moment that brought us this encounter speaks to us. It says via our conscience: "You have done wrong to this brother, this sister. Clear up what you recognize, so that something similar to what you have done to your neighbor does not happen to you. For you will reap what you sow."

May 16

Indecision brings inner conflict

How will you decide: for the truth, for Christ—or for the world, the illusion? Both simultaneously is not possible. Jesus said analogously: For or against Me. Once for the world, then again for Christ—that cannot go well in the long run. We become torn and remain torn until we decide.

Each of us must decide anew each day. This also requires courage and strength every day anew, until we feel the nearness of God. Then it becomes calmer and quieter, and we live more consciously in God.

May 17

God never forsakes you. Turn back!

Dear brother, dear sister, should you not succeed in some things, then when the "old Adam" breaks through again, for example, your old disparaging, envious and self-opinionated thoughts, then know that: God never leaves you. If you become aware of your sinfulness, turn back! In your thoughts, ask your fellow people for forgiveness for the negative things that you have sent to them, and at the same time also forgive them, if you suspect that they are thinking the same or similar things.

However, the most important point thereby is that you recognize your point, your part. Clear this up and no longer do it. In this way, you make peace with your neighbor in your inner being.

May 18

The key to goodness is not turned by rules

We have become accustomed to imposing rules on our fellow people. Only the fewest people are aware that the key to goodness is not turned by rules, rather we unlock the gate to life by living God-consciously.

May 19

Begin the day in the awareness: I am a child of the light

One help for the day would be to start it in the awareness: "I am a child of the light." If we cannot yet fully affirm this absolute statement, then we could affirm God's light, His power, His kindness and His love, in us.

Then we should also become aware of the reality of this power when situations come to us that we are not able to cope with right away. If correspondences awaken, we might briefly go within and affirm God's light, His power, His kindness, His love and His help in us.

We now wait a few moments—and then tackle the situation with the question: What does it want to tell me? What in me can I now dissolve, that is, transform, with Christ?

May 20

Become an optimist who does everything with the positive power in all things

Let's put our feelings and thoughts on the scale of our feelings to find out whether we are oriented positively or more negatively, in other words, whether we are an optimist or a pessimist.

Pessimists have a much harder time in life, because they see many things as gray in gray.
On the other hand, optimists always let the sun shine through the gray, because despite the clouds they do not focus on the gray, the negative. They affirm the good, that is, the light; they affirm the fulfillment of what they have set out to do that is positive.

Pessimists think of failure, disappointment, and being unsuccessful: "I'm a disaster. Everything will go wrong again today." Such negative programming works; many things do in fact go wrong, because we have input it.

On the other hand, optimists affirm the positive, also in the negative, because they know that the good is in all things. They try to find this in every situation. Their smile says: "No matter what the day brings—it cannot do me in. I will manage it with the positive power in everything." Optimism holds some healthy cheerfulness, from which the inner life force radiates.

May 21

Inner restlessness indicates that an unpleasant matter wants to be brought to a good end by you

If you feel restless during the course of your day, if your irritation level increases, don't leave things as they are. Briefly analyze *why* you are restless and agitated. If you like, clear it up in your thoughts and make a note of what you can make amends for. Writing it down is like speaking it out, it makes it easier; you become calmer. When you have time for this later on, you can bring it to a good end.

The deed is the step that makes you free.

May 22

Do first for your neighbor what you expect from them. In this way, you will be free of bindings and dependency

In situations and encounters with our fellow people, we Original Christians have resolved to remember the principles of the Sermon on the Mount, one of the most important of which is: What I want and expect from my brother or sister, I will do first for them.

We have experienced how the fulfillment of this spiritual principle works: We become more dynamic; we feel how we gain in strength, how we become free of bindings and dependency and how this principle inspires us to take further steps in the fulfillment of the divine laws. They are steps into the life in the Spirit of God.

May 23

God is able to work in the person from the inner stillness

Self-recognition always starts from the central place of stillness, which lies in us, deep in the very basis of the soul of each and every person.

From the inner stillness, God, who is the stillness, can be active in the person. He conveys impulses to the quiet human mind, in order to draw the person close to Himself and lead the person into stillness and spiritual objectivity.

May 24

You attract only what is active in yourself

*W*holeness lies in ourselves.
We people long for the perfect world, for peace with our fellow people, for health and happiness. Mostly, we look for it in those people we think can give us what we are seeking.
Those who are looking for the perfect world, including health, peace and happiness, naturally do not possess what they are looking for. If they had these values, they would not be looking for them.
A divine law is: Like attracts like. In other words: You cannot attract what you do not have.
So we attract only what is active in ourselves.

May 25

Out of all negativity flows the positive—if you clear things up

Out of all negativity flows the positive. Take this positive aspect, and go into the day—and you will experience in your neighbor what you bear within yourself:

Christ, peace, harmony and happiness. Affirm this, and it will come to you—if not through people, then it will flows from your inner being.

May 26

We can learn from the misconduct of our neighbor

We learn from our own misconduct—and also from the misconduct of our neighbors, provided we do not disparage them. In this way, we gradually feel what peaceableness means; it knows no violence.

If we strive for peacefulness by clearing up with our fellow people what is pending, then we will gradually become wise. Wise people do not take weapons; they do not strike back. They do not want to distroy their neighbors, but to reconcile with them.

In the case of disputes, remember: Clearing things up brings peacefulness. Togetherness leads to oneness. Learning on oneself and from one's neighbor leads to an expansion of consciousness. Through this, we grow into God-consciousness, into His wisdom and greatness.

May 27

If some things go wrong – it doesn't have to stay that way!

If some things go wrong today—it doesn't have to stay that way! The day gives you the strength to put order in what is in disorder. Do this before the thoughts torment you. Do this before you take further steps that lead in the same direction of disorder. Clear it up right away, and you may be able to take a little restful nap at noon, for example, or to rest somewhere, in order to regain strength for more. Perhaps you will be able to immerse yourself for a few minutes in the depths of the basis of your soul, where there is stillness and calm and the invigorating power of the Christ of God.

May 28

Raise your consciousness in order to be a true Christian of the deed

In the morning, are you already carrying the spiritual palm of peace, positive, selfless thoughts and feelings—or the storm flag, the vacillating disposition, which in turn shows itself in feelings and thoughts?

The spiritual palm of peace means that you gradually raise your consciousness to be true servants of God—Christians of the deed who learn to understand their fellow people, who welcome them into their heart and weigh their behavior on the scales of righteousness. True servants are the good Christians who daily recognize their all-too-human aspects, their sinfulness, who clear them up and no longer do them.

May 29

What God thinks of you is important

For many years, a guiding principle has accompanied me, which is:
What the world thinks of me—that is, what my fellow people think of me—is all the same to me. In every situation, in everything that comes my way, I will ask God what He thinks of me.

May 30

Taking energy from our fellow people—or receiving energy from God?

How do you want to act today? Do you want the people to applaud, that all who see and are around you consider you the center? Or do you want to honor God, so that His will can be done through you?

A help for this day: Will is the element of water and thus, movement, the "Let there be." Either our ego-will or else God's will in us sets in motion what we think, speak and do today. Thus, each one of us has the free will to put the ego into action in thoughts, words and deeds or to surrender to God's will, in order to clear up today and every day what constantly bothers us, what agitates us again and again, what tenses our nerves so that we often see our neighbors only in the spotlight of our ego-will.

May 31

Recognize yourself in the stillness of your heart as part of the eternal Being

To achieve a friendly conversation with our fellow people means to communicate with God.
To enter into communication with God means to become still. It is in the stillness of the heart that we recognize ourselves as part of the eternal Being.

June 1

Possibilities, for letting the senses, the nerves and the disposition become calm

If we find it very difficult to conclude a difficult situation, then it is advisable to take a few steps into nature or to linger for a few minutes at an open window, that is, to look out consciously, to let our eyes feast on the green of the tree, the bush or the meadow. Green calms and harmonizes the nervous system.

There are many possibilities for letting our senses and our mind become calm. Often it is merely a friendly smile that comes from the heart, a greeting directed to our neighbor, a considerate word for our brother, for our sister—so many things help us to reflect and become calmer.

June 2

Never strictly say "no." There is a solution in everything

It is good to never strictly say "no" right away. The word "no" is something closed; it does not allow anything more. Remember: There is a solution in everything. For example, find the positive in every opinion of a fellow person. Contribute it, and you will never bluntly say "no," but will have a solution. In this way you serve God and do not indifferently face your neighbor with a limiting "no."

No matter how the day goes, you always have it in hand to clear up some things or to rejoice in what went positively. Know: There is always a solution. The moments are precious. Many things can be resolved in a minute, so that we are again balanced, thankful and happy.

June 3

Get rid of what pressure and malaise want to tell you

If you are not completely satisfied with your day, if you still have some things to do—often you only feel this in the pit of your stomach, it is a kind of grumbling, something that creeps up on you, but which cannot be grasped yet—a word of advice: go into heartfelt prayer, and ask Christ to help you reflect on yourself. You will feel many a thing moving in your heart. You may experience that this rises from the stomach area like pearls bit by bit and into your conscious mind—and you suddenly know what the pressure and the malaise want to tell you. If you have recognized it and if the will to clear it up is present, then it can also be cleared up quickly, and the new, the good, can enter your life. If you do this, you will become more trusting in God, more peaceful and will gain powers of harmony.

June 4

Attract what makes your daily life invaluable

*E*very day we set barriers for ourselves through our sinful thinking, indeed, through all our sinful behavior.
Perhaps today will bring you some occurrences, in which you can recognize that you set barriers for yourself—barriers through jealousy, barriers through envy, barriers through every kind of egotistical behavior. Surely you can remove some barriers by recognizing and clearing up *your* part in the situation, in the occurrence, in the arguments.

The moment we remove the barriers—of course, with the help of the Lord, because without the help of the Christ of God nothing works—we already feel the inflow of the Spirit, of the divine fullness. Our disposition becomes lighter and more buoyant. We feel, as it were, an updraft to higher and purer shores.

What we send, we attract. What we clear up, we resolve and step by step enter the fullness of God. Then from the fullness of God, we attract what makes our daily life worthwhile.

June 5

Do not needlessly move in thoughts what is bothering you. Make use of the time!

We often say: I can't fix so quickly what's bothering me now.—But isn't that usually an excuse? Because then, when we become aware of it, we are also given a certain amount of time to clear up what has affected us—unless we move it around in our thoughts longer than necessary and let the time to clear it up pass. Then we rightly say we have no time now.

The time span of our life on Earth has many moments. We should make use of them!

June 6

With God's help make the best possible of your life

Every person is their own lawmaker. Depending on what we have entered in our soul, we experience joy or suffering.

If we remember that we are transmitters and receivers, we realize that every day, indeed, every hour, even every moment, is significant. And Christ is with you, the Great Helper, the greatest caregiver, the greatest love. So those who have courage, who tackle things and don't avoid obstacles gain joy. If you like, take the following with you into the hours of this day:

With God's help, we can make the best possible of our lives. If we are role models in this respect, we will be understanding and well-disposed toward our fellow people; we will make peace and keep peace.

June 7

Your hours could become building blocks of a brighter future

Remember: You are the thought. You are the hour, and in the hour lies the insight for you to turn around, to make many things better. Or will you leave everything as it is, that is, let the hour prevail, so that it transplants itself into the future with all that it bears as oppressive and burdensome aspects, in order to come again?

It is up to you to make your future and thus, your fate, brighter and friendlier. If you want to make use of the chance, think about your hours today. They can decipher much for you and become the building blocks of a brighter future.

June 8

Make peace with your neighbor and you will also have peace with yourself

Your irritations are your correspondences. They lead to restlessness and a disturbed body rhythm. Perhaps you already feel something like this in the morning?

If you want to, clear up the restlessness of the heart and go into the day feeling calm and cheerful. Thus, make peace with your neighbor in your heart, and you will also have peace with yourself.

June 9

The breath of nature refreshes you and calms you

When we step out into nature, for a while we leave behind the restlessness, the many impressions in the apartment, in the house, so that we can breathe life and absorb the forces of life. They refresh and strengthen us and calm us.
If you want, try it. You will experience that God surrounds you, and you will experience what it means to think little and speak even less, that is, to live reflectively.
Go into the day with the forces of nature, and you will experience yourself in a completely different way: more prudent, happier, uplifted, secure.

The breath of nature brings us prudence, inner happiness, peace and security.

June 10

Fulfill with heart and head what the day brings you

Everything we tackle just with our head, with our intellect, are tasks or questions that are difficult to cope with or answer. For example, our work is going slowly; conversations do not bring the desired success; colleagues are grumpy; and you become tired, perhaps overwhelmed and resigned.

However, if the day arrives in your heart, then your work goes easily and well; conversations are meaningful and promising. You can give your colleagues friendly and encouraging words for their day, so that a good working atmosphere develops.

Ask yourself more often who is in charge of the day: The others? Situations and events? Or yourself?

June 11

Find the light, which also shines in the dark: Christ, the present in all things

*N*on-recognition leads to error. You have surely already experienced this.

Those who do not explore themselves do not know themselves and will not know their neighbor either, because they look solely at the shadows and do not find the light that also shines in the shadow: Christ, the present in all things.

June 12

Detoxify your soul and your body. Initiate a turnaround in your life

Make use of this day, because it is a gift from God, so that you may recognize a part of your egoistic inputs, and then clear them up with the help of the Christ of God and no longer do them, so that your feelings and thoughts become more and more peaceful, selfless, unifying. Then you also fill your organism with the law of love. Your organs will thank you for this, because you detoxify your soul as well as your body, and in your life you contribute to the reconciliation of people, just as you reconciled with your neighbor. In this way, you take the chance to initiate a turnaround in your life.

June 13

To please God—
or your fellow people?

*P*erhaps a daily impulse for you as well: Do you want to please God or people?
What good does it do you to please people? What do you get out of it when they praise you and appreciate you? It's like a phantom—it rustles and is gone in a moment.

Accept this day and be aware that what is important is that we are accepted *by God*, that God loves us, because from this comes peace, freedom and happiness for us.

June 14

Peace with yourself— peace with your fellow people

Our day begins well when we live in peace with our fellow people. This shows us that we also have peace with ourselves.

We achieve peace by closing the day well in the evening and, with the help of the Christ in God, our Father, clearing up everything that we are aware of that is not nice—that is, when we clear up everything that we have felt, thought and spoken unkindly, disparagingly and spitefully— by asking for forgiveness and forgiving and no longer doing it. Then, during the night, while we are deeply asleep, higher powers flow to us and first thing in the morning, we gladly and joyfully enter the guidance of God, our heavenly Father.

June 15

Positive communication creates the equilibrium between soul and body

If after our day's work we say with relief: "Finally, the day is coming to an end, it's closing time," then something is wrong in our world of thinking. However, if we can say, "The day's work is done," then we have been focused, we have worked consciously and were in good communication with our work, with our colleagues and with our supervisor. Positive communication—no matter where the day takes us—brings about a balance between soul and body and ultimately, also tranquility for the soul.

June 16

Your day—a day of grace. If you change your thinking today, shadows will become light

The negative energies we have input announce themselves by knocking on our heart, touching our conscience. Thus, our sinfulness warns us before it breaks into our lives and becomes our fate. Therefore, we have the opportunity to recognize our bad way of feeling and thinking.

If we change our way of thinking today, shadows will become light. We are given this chance every day. This makes each day a day of grace.

June 17

You will reap what you sow

In the morning, many a one thinks negatively about this new day, "Oh dear, another one of those days! I am tired of the troubles and efforts I see coming my way."

Why give up on the day in the morning when you don't know what it will bring?

You will say, "What will the day bring me but hassles and difficulties?" Ask yourself *who* will bring you these difficulties, *who* will cause you trouble. You have made the difficulties for yourself, and the day will point them out to you again. They are the innumerable useless and unloving thoughts you have thought: harmful thoughts toward people or thoughts about your own advantage, disparaging thoughts, thoughts of your own upgrading, or even thoughts of weariness of life that arise from the previous thoughts. These are negative thoughts, ego-thoughts.

You have it in your hand to sow the good today.

June 18

No sinner need despair

No sinner need despair. If we have fallen, we can get up at any time and continue our way to the higher life, "Nearer, My God, to You."

If this day begins for you with negative thoughts such as envy, belittlement, anger or even fear of the coming day, of your colleagues at work, of your boss, then know: In everything and in everyone is God. No sinner need despair.
Perhaps these words will help you. If you go deeper into them and measure your thoughts on them, then you will know what you can clear up with Christ already in the early morning, so that your view will rise again and you will go into the day with hope and confidence.

June 19

God hears and understands you. He is the power of light and of love in you

Through a deep, meditative prayer, you can see many things more clearly and take in the finer vibrations. Even if they are only nuances of higher light vibrations—you may experience what it means to strive higher, to go, as it were, into the inner being, to God, who accompanies you throughout the day. Be aware that also now He is with you—He, God, your, our, Father, the power of light and love in you.

As the day draws to a close, close the day in heartfelt communication with God in you.

Become aware that He hears and understands you. Speak to Him from your heart and you will receive the answer—not in words, but in your feelings. Suddenly you feel a breath of peace, of happiness, of joy, of something extra-earthly, which this world does not know.

That is the answer of God, our Father, to His child. It is the glad tidings of love; because God wants a cheerful and joyful child that devotes itself to Him every day anew.

June 20

The content of your feelings, sensations, thoughts, words and actions have an effect— you are responsible for it

We cannot compare or even equate ourselves with anyone; nor can we make ourselves the same as them, because the content of each person's feelings, sensations, thoughts, words and actions is different. As a result, in all things we are dependent on ourselves.

According to the law of free will, each person is responsible for the course of their life. Everything is energy. And even if we conceal from others what is going on inside us, that is, what we secretly feel, sense and think—it is nevertheless energy that acts and has an effect, and we are responsible for it.

June 21

Awaken in your innermost being. Sense the brotherhood with ever more people

If you like, take some help with you into the day:
Whenever you meet a stranger and you suddenly sense a feeling of inner kinship, you can say, "I am awakening in my innermost being, for I feel a sense of brotherhood with more and more people, whether I know them or they are strangers."
Every stranger who stimulates our innermost feeling, which gives us a sense of kinship, of brotherhood in the Spirit of Christ, shows us that we are awakened in the light of the Lord.

June 22

Positive thoughts are positive powers; they come from God, the sun of life

If you feel well, that is, balanced, then the sun is already shining in your heart, which also shines for your neighbor.

Dear brother, dear sister, know that feelings and thoughts are powers. Positive, benevolent, constructive, sunny feelings and thoughts are positive powers. They come from God, who is the good, kindness, the sun of life.

God always radiates the good and helpful. Remain in His sun. If you like, then give thanks to this sun, which shines on you already in the morning. It is the source of life, the good, which makes you strong, joyful and happy.

June 23

In giving thanks you give yourself to the Christ of God and receive strength to deal with your day

If you are happy and glad when you review the past hours of the day, they certainly went well. Do not forget to give thanks.
Giving thanks stimulates soul and person.
Give thanks even when hours of your day do not go so well and you may be very hectic. In giving thanks for all things, you give yourself to the Christ of God. In thanksgiving you also receive the strength to recognize the actions that made you hectic and to clear them up.

June 24

The one who gives selflessly will receive

Selfless love awakens, in turn, selfless love. And what you receive from the selfless gifts, that is, what you gain, pass it on. If you go into the day in this awareness, you will also succeed in many things and will recognize what it means to live. The person who gives selflessly will also receive much.

June 25

The day, your friend, speaks to you

If you have accepted the day, your good friend, then it speaks to you—also through your family, through your friends, your colleagues, your boss. The day speaks to you while you drive to work in your car. It also speaks to you while you are working. It speaks into your thoughts, or it is your thought. What it tells you is you yourself, because you have input it this way during the past days.

June 26

What goes out from you goes back into you

If you succeed in bringing a little happiness to your neighbor, you will also feel happy and thankful. To bring a little happiness means to be kind, to stop thinking so often about our own well-being and to think more about the well-being of our neighbor.

If our neighbor is doing well and we have contributed to this, then we will also be doing well, because what goes out from us goes back into us. Clear up what is troubling you. You know how to do it. On the one hand, you can make a phone call; on the other, you can write a letter, or perhaps go to your neighbor to clear up what is still between you. If something needs to be cleared up in thought, do this quietly with Christ. Then it will also become quiet and calm in you.

June 27

If you help your soul, then you help yourself

The night has gone by. It is dawn.
Is it also dawn in your consciousness? Have you turned to God to thank Him for the small incarnation? Because your soul has returned—that is, you yourself—from other realms and is again in its body to spend its day, that is, your day, as a human being.
The soul knows that on this day it can clear up many things that its human being has inflicted on it. If you also realize this as a human being, then you will be able to help yourself, the human being, and also your soul very, very much.

June 28

Self-reflection brings rich fruits, if you overcome yourself and initiate the change

Self-reflection can make us aware of many positive aspects of our life, but also of the base things and tribulations of our life, which may have been weighing on our heart for a long time. Many will say, "Oh, you have to live with it. That's just the way it is."

Dear brother, dear sister, hold on to the positive sides of your life, and take hope, because everything can be clarified with Christ. If repugnant circumstances enter this day of your life, today is the day that gives you the strength to take the steps of clearing them up.

Self-reflection can bring rich fruits—if we conquer ourselves and initiate the change right away.

JUNE 29

Christ wants to make you happy. Do not look at your neighbor

Even if you do not succeed in everything right away, the good steps are decisive. They lead to a higher life, to freedom and happiness.

Many times we say in the morning, "Everything is so hard." What's the use of saying this? We don't change it thereby. We all think that we have it the hardest, that our neighbor or our colleague at work has it much easier.—Well, one has it harder, the other has it easier. What does it achieve if we think and ponder about it?

Don't look at your neighbor, because you don't know what he is bearing. You see only the shell, not the content.

Christ, however, knows each one of us. He wants to make us happy. Perhaps this would also be a consciousness aid for you: Christ wants to make you happy.

June 30

Self-observation and going within give you a good start in the day

How do you want to shape your day? Go into a short contemplation. Consider the good things you took with you from the previous day. Or go into a self-meditation by thinking your own meditative thoughts, that is, thinking them into your inner being. Then pray with all your heart. Thank God for your life on Earth, but also for your day, which holds many opportunities for you.

If there were some hours of sunshine during the past days, moments of reflection, minutes of happiness, perhaps you will also think about these sunny times and thank God.

And remind yourself of the good that has come about by clearing things up and overcoming the negativity. Bring to mind all the positive aspects, the principles of life that you have resolved for yourself. You have input them. Now they are effective, pointing out more to you and enriching your life.

The morning self-observation and going within give you a good start in the day.

July 1

Rectify the shadows via self-recognition. Be joyful and bring joy

How will you deal with today? You may say that there is something oppressive in you, as if there were a veil in front of your disposition. See, your feelings tell you what is hidden behind the veils. So take away the veil, the shadows. Look at yourself, at how you still are, and clear up your sinfulness.

You may say, "Many people are spiteful, disparaging, envious, cantankerous and argumentative." Many—you too?

If this upsets you, you also have traces of it. So remove the traces and bring joy! Make a firm resolve that your morning will be sunny. Inner joy lets you feel the inner breath of clarity and inner greatness. And realize: God is in you, your best friend, your companion and helper.

Therefore, go joyfully into the day. Stay joyful, even when you notice that something is moving behind the veils. You have the strength to clear this up, so that the day will stay sunny.

July 2

Keep in touch with the voice of your day. Strive for a conscious life in the present

It is good if you stay connected to the voice of your day, to the voice of your inputs. We often briefly lose it now and then.

If we get upset about a situation, about an event of the day, then we lose the alertness for our day and "lose," as it were, the voice of our day as well. But the moment we remember again that the day speaks to us, that we can hear the voice of our day—ultimately, our own inputs—we will remember ourselves again and thus, what the day wants to tell us in its moments and situations, to live consciously in the present.

July 3

Set your daily motto aglow; fill it with life by putting it into practice

Would you like to hear some good advice? Whatever you encounter today—put Christ first by remembering your day's motto, which can be, for example: "Only those who love God know that God loves them. Those who do not love God love the world."

Set your day's motto aglow, fill it with life by putting it into practice. Then God's love will glow through you more and more and be your sun and guiding star.
Explore yourself in this statement, and you will freely and joyfully carry out what you have set out to do.

July 4

The majority of people always wants to display themselves. You too?

Do you want the majority of people to accept you, or do you want to remain unrecognized?
Know that most people never know you, because they are not interested in you—only each one for themselves.
Those who move in the crowd think only about their base self again and again and in many cases have no access to their neighbor. Their acting skills are probably versatile, but they serve only to gain recognition, appreciation and the like. The majority always wants to display itself, so that each one of the majority—even if only for a short time—can be the center. That's what everyone is chasing after.

JULY 5

Don't let yourself go. Get going, and you will prevail with Christ

Let's put ourselves on our own test bench to examine our thoughts and words. If we look at the content of our thoughts and words and figure out whether they truly serve toward our perfection, whether they bring us happiness, contentment and perhaps also health, we will recognize some things in and about ourselves that we can change.

If you think about it just a few times, you will experience that just the attempt is a gain and is encouraging in the awareness: I will not let myself go. I'm tackling it and will be victorious with Christ.

July 6

Live *in* the day, in the awareness that God is the life

If we live *in* the day in the awareness that God is the life, we will also orient ourselves toward this life and increasingly ask about the commandments of this life, which God is. If you fulfill God's commandments step by step, then in the evening you can say that you have truly made use of the day. Then the coming days will be more light-filled, for what is cleared up today is also cleared up in the future—and even farther. Then you sense how you increasingly find inner stillness.

A consciously lived life also includes a daily plan and an honest daily review in the evening. The review helps you to remain or become more confident, and to consciously and thoughtfully spend the evening more quietly. Among other things, this results in good conversations that reveal many things that were previously hidden from us.

July 7

The sun is high, the radiation is strong; the help is great

God is the sun of life.
Do you want to go through your day with a cheerful disposition? Then always apply the affirmation of love, of light and of peace from God. If you not only think or speak out these words, but fill them with faith and hope, you will not only be hopeful, but also cheerful. If there are still some clouds on the horizon—if you like, you can clear them around noontime or in a brief quiet minute.

Dear brother, dear sister, the sun is high, the radiation is strong, the help is great. And if you clear up the remaining clouds now, you will enter the day more serene, more joyful, more hopeful, indeed, even cheerful.

July 8

Every breach of the law is self-love, which brings suffering and sorrow in its wake

Do not transgress the laws of life, for every breach of the law is self-love, which brings suffering and sorrow in its wake.

Every sinful thought we nurture is a force that goes out from us. It also comes back to us loaded with those effects that we sent out as causes. Every sinful thought is thus against the law of eternal love and already has in its wake what it contains. What thoughts are troubling you now? They have specific contents that now manifest themselves to be solved, that is, cleared up. The power of the Christ that dwells in you helps you do this. If we do not clear up in time what is pending, then what has toubled us today will come back to us at some point.

July 9

Thank God for the finished as well as the unfinished, and you will feel new courage

If you do the things you have intended and do your work calmly and with concentration, you will feel joy. Inner joy has a positive effect on your further work and also on your co-workers.

As soon as you feel disquiet, ask yourself: What does this disquietude want to tell me? Make yourself aware of this. Clarify and clear it up in your inner being. Perhaps make a note of it so that later you can put it in order externally. If you want, place everything, what is finished as well as not finished before God, our Father, the good power in all things.

Give thanks for everything. Then you will feel the fresh courage and creative energy that He has given and gives you.

July 10

Your words are shells, husks; it depends on their content

Words can be compared to husks that we fill with what we feel, sense or think while speaking. This morning it could certainly be of interest to you what you felt, sensed or thought when your first good morning greeting came over your lips. What we fill the shells, the words, with, their meaning, that is decisive, that is a part of our life on Earth. That is namely we, ourselves. With this, we have shaped our body. It is also a part of our inputs in the cosmic computer, in the memory network of the purification planes and the material cosmos.

So the content of our words also determines the life of our soul in the worlds of the beyond after our physical death.

July 11

Being exalted by our fellow people—what do we gain from this?

We always want to control our neighbors, if possible, so that they say what we want to hear, so that they praise us, so that they speak favorably about us. But what do we gain from this? Does it make us more content, more peaceful, happier, healthier and stronger? Or do we always fall back into the craving for recognition, for being exalted and the like?

If we want to tackle the problem of wanting our ego confirmed, let's ask ourselves: What do we gain if one or two people praise us? Are their words really filled with honest esteem? Are the contents of the words we hear really as positive as they seem? Only then, when we make a daily effort to gradually live according to the commandments, will we soon not care what people think of us. Our concern will be how God sees us.

July 12

You determine the course of your day in the morning

The first thoughts, feelings and sensations tell us how our night was and where our soul was.
If we woke up calm and harmonious, the past days were also reasonably positive. Our soul was able to go to higher regions of light during the night and build itself up there. If the past days were hectic, if we were often "beside ourselves," then our soul is burdened; it does not have the energy to go to higher, lighter spheres at night and

it reflects its burden to us already in the morning. Our first morning hours often determine the rest of our day. Our thoughts, feelings and sensations give, as it were, the starting signal for a whole series of dissonances, if we do not immediately clear things up and prescribe spiritual principles of life to ourselves.

If our thoughts are balanced, this is the basis for an orderly and balanced course of the day.

July 13

Rely on God and do what is right

During the day, it is worth looking at what is pressing and hectic to find out what it consists of. If you can't immediately take care of what is pending—unfinished business or problems and difficulties—then write down your intention: Once you have written out what you want to clear up, it will be easier for you.

You can include clearing up the pressing thoughts in your daily plan—with whom you want to talk, where you want to bring clarity into a matter.

When you formulate a positive sentence that you enter into yourself, you gain some distance from the hectic and the nervousness. The hectic thoughts may creep up on you even though you have put them down on paper. A consciousness aid would be: "I rely on God and do what is right." All this takes only minutes.

Then, in prayer, place in God's hands the disquiet that is still present. Entrust yourself to God and know that you are in His kind hands, that He wants to guide and lead you.

July 14

Everyone can find spiritual freedom, the freedom in God

Again, a new day announces itself. Again, personal thoughts come and with them either lightness or heaviness.

Many a person will sigh and say, "Oh, again the work, again the confinement, again the coercion!" Can work be coercion if we live in God? God is freedom, and spiritual freedom, the freedom in God, can be found by everyone when they inwardly detach themselves from what still ties them down.

July 15

Tranquility and a sunny heart bring a sun-filled day

There should be tranquility, tranquility, above all, in our thoughts. If we have the necessary tranquility, if our thoughts are largely in harmony, if we feel at one with our neighbor, then it is a sunny day, even if the sun is covered by clouds, even if the clouds are raining down.

The heart is important. A sunny heart is also one with the elemental forces of fire, water, earth, air. Being one with the elements means being in communication with the forces of creation.

July 16

Your past is your present. Shall it also be your future?

What upsets us wants to tell us something. We encountered something, a person, a situation. We reacted angrily, disappointed, unwillingly, with envy or the like. What happened? Our soul was stimulated, and the reaction shows what we once entered into our soul and into the cosmic memory. Every moment is rich in content. It brings many thoughts and feelings. It stimulates situations and problems—or it brings, for example, the feeling of harmony and awareness of God. Both are possible, so it depends on what we have input during our life or during past sojourns on Earth.

Our past is our present, that is, the day, and the future, the forthcoming days. How do you want to deal with it now?

July 17

Through a pure life, you will be understanding, patient and benevolent

The movements in our life are always, above all, about our relationship with our fellow people. So with whom are you still not completely at peace? Clear that up immediately—if you want to; because you always have the freedom to do things one way or the other. If there is also something to be cleared up externally, you can call the person concerned or otherwise initiate the solution.

What else is pending? If you have done everything in your power, then tranquility and peace will pass through your disposition. After all, a good conscience is "a comfortable pillow." By living a pure life, we become more understanding, patient and benevolent. We will also allow our fellow people more and more freedom and in this way become free ourselves.

July 18

Dissolve the secrets of your past

One day has many minutes, many moments, many situations, many encounters. Your day brings you many a thing. Has it already revealed to you one or two secrets from your past today that you can clear up?

After clearing this up, we have a good feeling, a clear conscience; we feel freer and lighter than before. The worries and pressures that the uncleared thoughts made us feel have left us. We feel inner calm, warmth and vigor. This is the response to us of the Christ of God in us.

July 19

Don't torment yourself for long with distressing thoughts—remove them!

Possibly you say you lacked the time this morning to clear up your tormenting thoughts of denigration, envy or even fear. If we are willing, there are always possibilities! You go to your bathroom to cleanse yourself externally and get ready for the day. While you are grooming yourself externally, groom yourself internally at the same time. This way you can save time. If you are traveling by car and get in a line of traffic, you have to wait for a long time. Here, too, it is possible to clear up what the morning has already signaled to you. Or you are underway on foot. Some things can also be recognized and remedied thereby.

Know that the best teacher is in you. He knows about all things. He knows your day. Entrust yourself to Him, and the day will be a good day.

July 20

What agitates us is the correspondence in us

Become aware of what the movement in your life consists of. Do not look at the external alone—look deeper and examine *yourself*. What moved you and still moves you? What possibly annoys you about your neighbor? That is, what got you all worked up? Recognize that, and then see whether what disturbed you so much in your neighbor is not also present in the same or like way in yourself. It would not annoy you so or even agitate you, if it were not in you!

Therefore, find out what is in you—not in your neighbor! Only this is of importance for you, because: You can change yourself, but not your neighbor. He decides for himself how he wants to act.

July 21

Call on God even in all adversity—He is with you

God is in me just as in you. He is in each one of us. If we ask for God's help in everything that comes our way, if we feel His help now and then, we become more and more aware that God is with us, that He is very close to each one of us.

In every difficulty, in every situation, God, the power and help, can be experienced. You may address God in all things, also in every problem, in every difficulty, in everything adverse. We can become a completely different person because we have felt God's nearness, His unending love.

July 22

The free choice

The children of God, we human beings, are called upon to clear up the negative seed, the not-good, with our Redeemer, Christ, through His power and with His help, to remove it from the field of our life. We promote the good seed, our good, uplifting, positive, divine thoughts, by becoming aware again and again of the commandments of God and of the Sermon on the Mount. We measure our thinking and living against these spiritual principles and decide how we want to do things.

As children of God, we have free will. We have the choice. What do we choose?

July 23

To be silent at the right time

If you can be silent at the right time, you can find the solution in the situation and events of the day. If you have spoken the truth, then you are glad. You feel uplifted and strengthened by the inner power. Do not forget to give thanks for this. If you have not always succeeded in being silent at the right time, you should not be displeased. The situation wanted to tell you something personally, and you know what you can clear up.

July 24

Making a positive life program

Negative thoughts that draw our attention to the seeds in our soul should not be nurtured; but rather, they should be cleared up with Christ and we should endeavor to no longer think in the same or like way.

We can do this most easily if we become aware of how we want to think and act instead, from now on. By making a firm resolution, we enter a principle into our new, positive life program. We firmly hold on to this when we are tempted to fall back into the old mistakes, into the old negative way of thinking and acting.

JULY 25

If you trust God, you create confidence in Him

All the hours of our day should find fulfillment in His Spirit. Therefore, be aware that wherever you go—God's love and help go with you. Whatever may come your way—God is *for* you. God helps you at work, because He, the omnipresent power, is with you at work. God is also in your activity. God, the power and help, is in your conversations; He is in every encounter.

If we trust God, we create confidence in Him. If we call on Him in every situation, then we experience His help and feel His presence.

July 26

A day rich in experience: Look at yourself from a certain distance

It's amazing how often we humans pass ourselves by and do not even grasp what's going on inside us, and thus do not recognize who we are! If we want to put aside our humanness, that is, our sinfulness, then we have to look at our own thinking and doing from a certain distance. Would you like to once try this?

Whenever you get upset or angry with your work colleague, with the boss or a passerby, don't think about them for long, but look at your own thoughts and actions—and you will often feel disconcerted about yourself. How will you behave then?

That is up to you, because you have free will.

July 27

Turn to God, your Father; recognize the step that you can take today

If we engage in self-observation, in self-exploration, we are often amazed at our own feelings and thoughts—some of which run within us without our being aware of them—or at our words that we simply blurt out every day.

Clear up what makes you uneasy, whatever still needs to be cleared up, and place it into God's hands. God knows the answer and solution also for your questions and difficulties. If you turn to Him, your Father, you will recognize the step you can take today.

July 28

Use the moment, the present

What strongly affects and upsets us, what tenses our nervous system, what we think over and over again, that is still present. It urges us to analyze it briefly and clear it up—before it recedes into the past to return at some point, because nothing is lost, neither the positive nor the negative.

If we analyze our feelings and thoughts, we realize: Many seed corns are good, others less so. We should give thanks for both the positive and the negative, and clear up the less good with the help of the Christ of God in us.

Every seed of a thought or word eventually sprouts. Let us not think about it for long now, so as not to revive it again.

July 29

We are also responsible for our fellow people

We cannot put any blame or responsibility on our fellow people for what we do or do not do. Therefore, you can rightly say, "I am always responsible for myself!"

On the one hand, yes, but on the other hand, we are also responsible for our fellow people, namely through our positive or negative attitude. If, for example, we go to our friends with a negative attitude, then we can trigger many things in them through unkind or even nicely colored words or through our incensed, reproachful attitude, for which then *we* are jointly responsible.

On the other hand, a positive attitude leads to a positive, unifying conversation. In this way, we can also stimulate the positive in our neighbor, and thereby be a help to them on their journey through life.

July 30

The true art of living

A little help for this day—perhaps also for all future days:
Learn to master your thoughts and you learn to concentrate. And once you have learned to master your thoughts, they will obey you. This is the true art of living.

July 31

Find God, the happiness, in you

A sister, an Original Christian, who has experienced much, endured much and found inner strength would like to share something with you. If one or the other thought speaks to you, then it may have something to say to you.

My motto for every day is: Neither misfortune, worry nor suffering bring me to my knees, for God is my support and my staff. Even external well-being and external happiness do not impress me, because I have found God in me, the beauty, tranquility, stillness and peace. That for me is happiness.

August 1

Gain predominance over your thoughts, words and actions by being still

In being still, we also acquire predominance over our thoughts, words and actions. We are less and less dominated by our all-too-human aspects. Instead, we prevail more and more over ourselves. Thus, we take into our hands the rudder of our ship of life, in order to steer toward the primordial stillness that is God, the Intelligence in us. In time, we then also experience in and on ourselves the difference between intelligence and intellect.

Therefore, become still in order to then be still.

August 2

Christ helps us to work off our guilt in the law of sowing and reaping

We reap what we have sown; there is no escape—only Christ, who helps us to work off what we have been guilty of. The divine law, love, remains for eternity. Therefore, every violation of the divine law must be resolved.

If we are alert, during our day we always become aware of some of our inputs that contain fatal traits, for example, thoughts of disparagement, the feeling of spitefulness, envy or sensations of additional unkindness. You now have a chance to clear up what you have now recognized and no longer do it. Then the violation of the law cancels itself out, because you fulfill the laws of love and are thus led step by step nearer to the origin of your life, which is present.

August 3

True happiness always comes from the heart, from the kingdom of the true Being

Do you do your day's work solely with your intellect or with your heart and head? Your mood tells you! Exuberant joy or dejection are often signals that we have responded and reacted to the moments, occurrences and situations of our day with the head, that is, intellectually. Inner joy, like thankfulness, and inner serenity, like being relaxed, are answers from the heart.

However, if your heart is heavy, if you are disgruntled and irritated, then it would be better to work out what oppresses you. Then you can decide whether you want to clear up with the help of the Spirit of God, of the inner kingdom, what is pending and what makes you disquiet. In doing so, you will again become aware that the Inner Kingdom is the eternal Being and that we are ultimately sons and daughters of this kingdom, eternally. There is our eternal being—here only a conditional existence.

The inner kingdom is the kingdom of the heart, which we also open only with the heart.

August 4

God guides you via the daily impulses, but also via your plan for the day

The impulses that want to speak to you about your feelings and thoughts help you to cope with the day. They help you to possibly clear up what needs to be cleared up. But they also help you to say a heartfelt thank you to God, our eternal Father, for the day.

Surely you have a plan for the day and perhaps a plan for the week. Become aware of your plan, especially in the morning and evening, and place it in God's hands so that He can guide you through the day or week.

August 5

Get to know yourself in the content of your words, so as to understand your neighbor

Everyone puts different feelings, sensations and thoughts into their words. We may hear what the individual is saying, but we do not know the content of the words spoken to us. That is why there are so many misunderstandings and often arguments. The first step would be to first get to know the content of our own words. Ask yourself: What have I put into my words? Based on your self-recognition, you will gradually come to understand your neighbor better. If you often get to the bottom of the words spoken, you may realize that we often speak past one another or that some things were not meant in the way we think we "understood" them. If we would realize this, then there would be less discord and quarrelling, and it would be easier to live with each other.

August 6

Pressing wanderlust—how is the state of your soul's freedom?

Your soul is underway every night. It goes on its paths of consciousness created by you, which you have predetermined by your way of feeling, thinking and wanting. Thus, it goes into planes or realms that we as human beings cannot reach. As long as we human beings feel the urge to travel around, to see and enjoy other countries, we have not yet paved the way to higher realms for our soul, but have more or less shackled it to our desires, so that when its body sleeps deeply at night, it is able to travel only a short stretch of consciousness because it cannot go farther. On this short distance, it can fetch only little life energy, so that the human being remains hungry for life.

August 7

Become aware of an inner travel destination; plan your inner journey

As long as our heart is unsettled and our soul is not yet able to seek out the vastness of infinity, we are striving for external pleasures and for as much as possible, ever more, ever more. No sooner are we back from vacation, than we are already planning the next one. On the other hand, we rarely plan the inner destination.

Every morning, planning for the inner destination would be good, for example, to become more peaceful and happy through the daily step-by-step fulfillment of the Ten Commandments of God, by keeping peace also with our neighbors, being with them and for them, by conscientiously doing our work and conscientiously using the day for our existence on Earth.

August 8

Recognize and clear things up in good time!

*A*ccept this day! It speaks to you. It is the grace of God that admonishes you to recognize in good time these and those sins, this and that seed that wants to sprout, to clear them up and no long do them.

If you like, listen to the day. And if you clear things up, in the evening you will realize that it was a good, a joyful day.

August 9

The longed-for salvation is in you yourself

Salvation, the good, the truly positive, is in us, and we can activate it ourselves. We must therefore become active to unfold the positive, which is a divine principle of the law. For example, if we have developed the ideal world by giving our neighbor a feeling of connection and true togetherness, if we have developed the spiritual principle of health of the soul by daily with Christ repenting of our recognized sins, clearing them up and no longer doing them, then many a thing will also come into order in our body because the causes of every illness lie in our soul.

Or: If we are happy in the awareness that the eternally loving God, the Father of us all, wants the best for us, and if we also behave in this way toward our fellow people, then our life will bring us more and more joy and we will succeed in many a thing.

August 10

The plan for truth— the guideline for your life

If you have made a plan for truth, then write it down. Whenever doubts come over you or you become negligent, keep to your plan for truth. Read it to yourself and bring to mind your words, your input.

Truth brings clarity and peace in you. The truth is always uniting. It does not exclude any person because truth is the same as unity.
Be aware that deep in their souls all people you encounter today are a part of your soul.
How do you meet this, your part?

August 11

You determine the rhythm of your day yourself

Already in the morning we determine the rhythm of our day. That is why we should quickly clear up not nice, hectic thoughts that want to impel and urge us. As a result of this hectic feeling, as a result of our pressing thoughts, we can make mistakes at work. If we give free rein to our pressing thoughts, by midday we are often already exhausted, nervous and stressed. Due to this imbalance, we react more violently than usual, are more impatient and ill-tempered and easily get into arguments with our neighbor. Looking back, we then realize: It started in the morning with our restless, hectic thoughts. Thus, if such thoughts already afflict you in the morning, it would be good to take a closer look at them, analyze them and clear them up, in order to start the day more calmly and balanced and to make the best of every situation.

August 12

From the awareness of being a child of God, grows inner joy and warm-heartedness

If you consciously closed the day last evening and cleared up the things that were not yet cleared up, then you surely slept well and will start the new day in a balanced way.

Make use of the quiet morning hour to direct a calm, meditative prayer to God, our Father. If we start the day in this way and think from time to time during the day of what we have prayed, then gradually the inner wealth awakens and we feel ourselves as children of God. Then inner cheerfulness and warmth of heart will determine the further days of our life.

August 13

Active faith gives us spiritual dynamism— a conscious, dynamic work in God's will

The day shows our behavior. Do we expect or give? Are we quiet and strong in faith in our inner being, or do we waver. Both—for and against—can happen to you; but one thing is certain: God loves you and He rejoices over you when you recognize the "against," clear it up with the help of the Christ of God and decide for one or a few commandments of God, which you then carry out step by step.

To clear up the sinful aspects is the active faith that reactivates us, that, as it were, permeates and strengthens us, that also gives us spiritual dynamism for the day, that is, a conscious and dynamic work in God's will.

August 14

To live in God, selfless, divine thoughts are required

To live in God means to fulfill the works God. This requires selfless thoughts, that is, divine thoughts.

If you want, at the beginning of the day, make yourself aware that every useless, insubstantial and unloving thought, every thought that disparages your neighbor, every thought of your own advantage, every thought of weakness and fear, every thought of discouragement and not being fit for life leads to a separation from God. This is not life, but rather nothing more than vegetating. Decide to live!

August 15

The positive from the negative traits that were overcome is a good new course for you

Do not forget to also recognize the good, which you encounter in the hours of your day!

Know: The good is also in the negative. It comes to light when we overcome the negative. This positive, good thing is then an aspect in our life plan. We can make a note of it, that is, write it down, because that is how we want to think and act in the future. We want to continue to build on it. It is our new resolution, our good, new course ...

August 16

Via your nervous system, figure out in feelings what is present in you

How do you feel? Is there melody or dissonance in your heart? If there is dissonance, feel deeply into it; feel into it to figure out what was and is present in you.

Our thoughts can often deceive us. They deceive us on how good we were and are. But what does the feeling say? The feeling strikes, as it were, the tuning fork, whose vibration, whose sound, has an effect on our disposition and on our nervous system.

Just as we feel, so is our day too. Analyze the "tuning fork," your feeling, by way of the resonance of your nerves.

August 17

Your thoughts toward your fellow people mark you

The day's work lies before you. *How* it is done and with what feelings and thoughts is decisive. The thoughts that either relax or strain our nerves cause reactions in and on our bodies and determine our behavior toward our fellow people. The good, the truly sovereign and helpful as well as the aids that we can incorporate in our daily routine mark our face and determine our body posture.

The ill humor that our fellow people bring into a conversation, to which we react in an upset and intolerant manner, or on whom we even force our opinion, also mark our face and our attitude. If during the day we briefly look at our reflection in the mirror, then we see who we are and have the opportunity to make an inner and outer course correction.

August 18

Raising your consciousness by clearing up the debit aspects of your day

Measure the hours of your day on your own positive guidelines. How are you doing with it? You feel this yourself.

If you like, a piece of advice: Briefly analyze your day at noon and in the evening. What is your debit; what is your credit? Thank God for both. Clear up the debit as soon as you can. Where should you have acted differently? Where should you have changed your thinking? To whom should you have said the right thing? What should you have changed about the situation? Many questions to yourself. If you clear up some of the debit aspects, your consciousness will be raised and you will feel the joy of the credit side, the feeling of fulfillment in the heart.

August 19

Overcome annoyance and resentment. The joy of creating contributes decisively to the success of the day's work

The day can also bring annoyance. But through a deep meditative prayer you have the strength to look more closely at the resentment, to recognize your share and then to clear it up. The annoyance then disappears and creative joy comes in, which contributes decisively to the success of the day's work.

August 20

Organize your day joyfully, by thinking and doing what is positive

Each day can bring many joys, but also unpleasant things now and then, possibly suffering. If we give thanks for the joys and resolve to make the day ever more joyful by thinking and doing more and more positive things, then we will also be ever more grateful to God.

August 21

The nicest victory: defeating yourself

The picture you select as your plan in the morning will guide you through the day. How do you deal with difficulties? Do you master them with the Lord's strength, or do you still have adversities to clear up? Know that the solution is in all things. You will find the good solution if you call upon the kindness of God and walk in His paths. As encouragement for a conscious life and as a consciousness aid, you can, if you like, also decide for an old folk saying for yourself that says: "To defeat oneself is the nicest victory."

If you have a few quiet minutes for yourself now and then, bring to mind once again what you have planned for the course of the day. If your inputs are in accordance with God's law, that is, if they are selfless, then the high forces of life will assist you, strengthen and guide you.

August 22

Attain inner unity and the conscious link with Christ

We should analyze, think over and, as far as we are able, clear up what keeps our nervous system in a state of turmoil. You can always ask for forgiveness and forgive the soul of your neighbor through Christ. You can also write down what is moving you. Then you are writing about yourself. You put it down on paper and know what you want to say or how you want to behave in the next few days or what you can make amends for. Do not forget: The center is Christ. He is always our helper and companion, our good friend. Make peace in yourself, then you will also send peace to your neighbor. In this way, we attain inner unity and the link to the center—the conscious link with Christ.

August 23

Create "sunny days" that are due to a child of the light

For many of us the day is patchy—some clouds, then again sunshine. How could it be otherwise? The "sun" delights us, and the "clouds" tell us what still needs to be cleared up, so that there are more and more hours of sunshine and sunny days that are due to the child of light, which each one of us is in our inner being.

Especially because the hours of our days seem to be getting shorter and shorter, you should allow yourself a little bit of reflection every now and then to clear what the clouds are signaling to you. Clear out any uneasy or anxious feeling so that you can go on with your day calmly, prudently and cheerfully. The light of God, His sun, His strength, kindness and love are with you.

August 24

God guides me—
now and beyond death

A central theme has guided me for many years, and it says: I expect nothing for myself in this whole life. I also expect nothing beyond death. I know that God guides me in this life on Earth and beyond death.

This awareness gave and gives me devotedness to God, and so I can say: I have become calm and quiet.

Dear brother, dear sister, perhaps something of this thought will help you for this day and for your future life on Earth.

AUGUST 25

If we do not get tired of seeking, then we will find God

If we do not get tired of seeking God, if we then, when we have fallen, keep getting up and clearing up our sinfulness with Christ, we will find our way to God in us.

You will say, "But my many thoughts!" Know that we will become master over our thoughts only when we do not talk about them all the time, but recognize and clear them up and no longer do them. Then we empty our vessel of sinfulness, and strength and love flow in. Then we will also understand our neighbors, accept and receive them and be with them. This would be a task for every day, because when we understand our neighbor deep in the very basis of our soul, then we have also grown close to God.

August 26

The best teacher is in yourself: Christ

A small help for your day:
Heed your conscience. Your conscience helps you to recognize yourself. It also helps you to sense whether you have solved problems lawfully, that is, according to the Lord's commandments, or whether you are in harmony with your colleagues, whether you have had conversations without emotions, and other things.

The moments of the day are our lessons, and the best teacher is in ourselves: Christ.

AUGUST 27

Transform the storm warning flag into the palm of peace

If your feelings, sensations and thoughts are stormy toward your neighbor and toward what the day may not have brought yet, then recognize yourself in it. This is a sign from God, who wants to tell you: Clear up the stormy feelings, sensations and thoughts and transform the warning flag into the palm of peace.

Having a good guideline for the day is also decisive and helpful when the so-called storm is already blowing. A stormy day is usually a hectic day. If the storm subsides already in the morning, then the day can become very friendly.

You determine yourself the course of your day. Welcome the palm of peace and clear up the stormy feelings, sensations and thoughts; then you will experience a sunny day.

August 28

Experience yourself by immersing in the depths of stillness

Often we do not know what the beginning of the day or a dream or situation we are aware of want to tell us.

It is easier for us to get to the experiential world of our soul if we immerse ourselves in the depths of our soul after awakening or after getting dressed. We reach the depths of the soul with the help of meditative thoughts, which we pray down into the very basis of the soul, in order to enter into communication with Christ in us. This meditative prayer is also called immersion in the depths of stillness.

The noise of the day does not penetrate into the very basis of the soul. Nor is the possibly already restless morning in the very basis of the soul.

There is tranquility. There is peace. There is recuperation for soul and body. If you like, immerse yourself in the very depths of the soul. Pray down, as it were, into, the luminosity of the Christ of God, and place your thoughts and your new day, perhaps your dream, before Him.

After the meditative prayer thoughts, be completely still. Remain in the innermost part of the Being, in the very basis of your soul, and know: The luminosity of the Christ of God brightens your conscious mind, so that you learn what the thoughts of the morning, the dream or already emerging difficulties and disturbing situations want to tell you.

August 29

Let the light of God shine on you by striving to fulfill His will

In the often gray and gloomy everyday life, when you see everything as gray in gray and your disposition is clouded by gloomy clouds, remember: Above the clouds the sun is shining. As long as we look only at clouds, we are looking at opinions of people and we stay with the opinions of people. These are then the standard for us and have validity. However, if we blow away the clouds, as it were, and let the sun shine on us, then we look into the light and also let the light warm us and set us aglow, so that we ask ourselves again and again: What is the will of God? This is what I want to fulfill.

If you like, this could be a guiding thought for your new day. It's worth an attempt to turn the gray sky into a blue one.

August 30

God knows and loves you. The person of the masses does not know you; he loves himself

May you become aware: God knows you, and He cares about you. The masses do not know you. What good does it do for you to pursue their favor? Does it bring you the inner peace and fulfillment that we call happiness?

With these thoughts on this day, you will surely make your observations and self-observations, valuable experiences and self-experiences.

August 31

The no— or the positive solution?

During the day, be frequently aware of the fact that the "no" separates us from our neighbor. The solution creates access to our neighbor.

September 1

Immerse in the divine Being; become still and aware of God

Immerse yourself in the divine Being. Pray. Give thanks for the day, and clear up with God what needs to be cleared up. Then you become calm. Your breath deepens. Your heart beats evenly. Pressing thoughts give way. Thoughts and feelings of hope, of joy move in. You become still. You feel more God-conscious and go into the coming hours of the day like this.

Then we don't have to ask ourselves: How was the day? It was good because your heart is beating properly.

September 2

Every hour is interesting for those who strive for God

Every hour is interesting for those who strive for God. Their life becomes interesting because they explore themselves with Christ's help. Those who explore themselves know what is at the basis of their thoughts and words, but also of their actions.

Our feelings in particular are often more revealing than our thoughts and words. They tell us more clearly who we still are at this hour, and, at the same time, reveal aspects of our future, our coming fate.

In your days on Earth, you have felt, sensed, thought, spoken and done many things. All this comes again, because no energy is lost. If we are alert today, then we experience our past and can clear up what it shows us. How we deal with the energy of our day today will help determine our future.

September 3

If you are balanced, you will have a balancing effect

It is a principle of God: If we are balanced, we will also have a balancing effect in conversations and in situations that arise, because the powers that grow in us by clearing up our sinfulness and by actualizing the laws of God enable us to give. If you want, you can resolve positive things for your day, such as contributing to peace, harmony and happiness.

September 4

Be silent in thoughts. Receive the life in nature

Every day should also include hours of rest. Nature shows us every day what peace and quiet actually mean. Especially on quiet days, in the morning, when the hustle and bustle of the day has not yet set in and we hear nature breathe in the evening, it is the stillness that it promises us. Do you also want to hear it?

Then, take time to go out in the morning or in the night. Let nature surround you and be still. Be silent in your thoughts. Do not speak. Receive the life that is the life of all of us, GOD.

September 5

Your thoughts are energies. They have an effect— one way or the other

With what does the day begin? It already begins in the morning with our thinking; because our physical body is, so to speak, a body of thought. People think, think and think; they thus mark their body and also determine their days on Earth.

Your thoughts have an effect—one way or the other ...

September 6

Do not let go of the rudder of your life's ship

Are you in control of your thoughts? If our thoughts were like a rudderless ship that drifts once here and once there, then we as human beings would be without control and would be controlled.

Those who do not know how to control their thoughts cannot control their bodies either. And those who do not know how to control their body let go of the rudder of their ship of life.

September 7

Control your thought process— think positively!

Dear brother, dear sister, a meditative prayer awakens the positive forces that help and serve us to become aware of our thoughts, so that we can have control over our thought process.

Make use of the positive forces, bring them into your world of thinking, as it were. Think positively! Then your soul will recover, and you, the human being, will also feel this. The happiness and joy, that is, the tranquility of the soul, will also be your joy, the joy of a successful day.

September 8

Use the energy of Christ

The day comes to each of us differently. It brings us what sinful aspects we have entered in our soul in past times, but also in certain heavenly bodies—which will be the abode of our soul after the death of the body—for instance, unloving, envious thoughts, derogatory and wrong words as well as corresponding deeds.

You will perhaps say, "God's law, which is love and life, will take everything from me because Christ, the love, life and mercy, died for me, for all of us." Yes, He died as Jesus—but He brought us redemption. He gave and gives us His power, so that through His energy in us, we may release ourselves from our sins and fulfill, step by step and more and more each day, the laws of love and peace. If you have time, go briefly into inner contemplation. Pray from your heart. Rest in Christ's love, then you will gain strength for the day.

September 9

You are free to act this way or that

You must know that God gave free will to all of us. Thus, we are free to act this way or that. But if we prove ourselves to be a child of God by gradually fulfilling the commandments of life, then the days will become increasingly light-filled, the situations ever easier. Then we will also have the strength to master our problems with the help of the Christ of God.

I wish you a day in the Lord.

September 10

Open yourself to the present, which is God and your true life

The present, which is God and our true life, opens up to us as human beings only through effort. Due to our time—that is, the sequence of past, present and future—and as a result of our inability to forgive, we rarely live consciously in the now, in the present, and thus, in the trust in God. Rather, on the one hand, we are preoccupied with our unresolved past and, on the other hand, with the future.

We often wonder what the future will bring us. The answer is quite simple: The essence of our past will sooner or later determine our future. What we have put into our feeling, sensing, thinking, speaking and acting is the pictorial material for our future; that comes back to us—also today. What do you want to do with it?

September 11

Strength for the day by practicing inner stillness

Through the help of Christ, your Inner Helper and Advisor, you can solve many things with His power.

By immersing in the inner stillness, you gain the strength for the day, to fulfill your work conscientiously and carefully and to live in peace with your colleagues. Do you also understand your supervisor? He, too, is not yet perfect and has to struggle with his shadows—like you. He bears within the same forces as you, the powers of the Christ of God, the light that helps and guides.

September 12

Adhere firmly to the positive aspects you have achieved, and build more positive aspects onto them

It is worthwhile to consciously swim against the current of the all-too-human aspects that wants to take us along. For example, if we don't accept every negative thought, but instead take a closer look at it to recognize ourselves and find the positive in it, we will gain another little bit of strength, light, inner joy and lightness of heart.
Realize that if we remain in the negative, nothing positive can develop. Therefore, adhere to the positive aspects you have achieved and build more positive aspects onto them.

September 13

Take a step back in what you want; leave freedom to your neighbor

The high and luminous forces of Being can guide us through the day and lead us if we entrust ourselves to them, if we leave freedom to our neighbor, if we take back our all-too-human, that is, sinful, wanting that wants to pressure and control our neighbor, and recognize ourselves in it.

Whenever we want to impose something at all costs, we want something for ourselves. At the same time, this base human wanting is directed against our neighbor. Then we also cannot be led by God, because we are against our neighbors, wanting to have a determining effect on them and deprive them of the freedom of their thinking and wanting.

September 14

A conscious way of life through the devotion to God

If you can entrust yourself to God's guidance in respective situations and conversations, then you sense what it means to enter into communication with Christ. Then you also know what it means to gain trust in the great Spirit who never lets us down when we turn to Him.

Let us practice to consciously shape our life by asking ourselves: Do I entrust myself to God—or do I want to put through my desires, my ideas and my opinions? We recognize "His" and "mine" when we examine ourselves. If we truly surrender to Him, the great Spirit, in conversation and in situations, then we remain calm and clear. Our consciousness expands, and we suddenly have thoughts that we never had otherwise, and find ways and solution possibilities.

September 15

You never need to give up, because Christ always helps you

Do not say, "Lots is going wrong today." "I can't manage it!" Do not despair!
Know: In every situation there is a solution. What was not good today will be better tomorrow, if we want this. If we continue to rely on Christ, then we also know that we never need to give up, because Christ always helps us.

September 16

Inner self-reflection leads to balance

If you are in a hectic state, go, if you want to, into a short, quiet self-reflection. A prayer, even a few deep breaths and a few words or reflective thoughts, spoken to within, often help us to find peace. When the vibrations of our whipped-up nerves subside, we can often think more clearly again. Then we can also become aware of what went wrong today, and possibly why.

If in the evening we want to conclude our day with Christ and gain from our experiences, we will make notes about what still makes us uneasy, clear it up as far as it is still possible for us, in order to then be able to go to our family, to our friends, in a more balanced and harmonious way.

September 17

Nothing positive can develop from the negative

Have you awakened with heavy and worrisome feelings and thoughts that weigh you down?
You don't need to take these along into your day. Just a few minutes of reflection early in the morning can give you a positive start on the day, if you take the time to examine the negative thoughts more closely. It's up to you to decide whether or not you want to hold on to what's heavy—perhaps accusations against your fellow people. If not, use the minutes to clear what has upset you. In your thoughts, ask for forgiveness, forgive and resolve to think and act differently in the future. Therefore, turn around and be positive again.
Nothing positive can develop from the negative. So see to it that you transform the negative into the positive. The inner power of your heart, the power of Christ, helps you with this.

September 18

Do not become a slave to pressing desires

If needs and desires are affecting you, analyze them. Why do they pressure you? What do you want? If the needs and desires can be fulfilled, that is, if they are within your possibilities, use the golden mean and fulfill them. If you were to just push them aside, that is, continue to carry them around with you, then you would gradually become a slave to these needs and desires that are urging you more and more. When a desire is urging us, we become more and more demanding and "uncomfortable"; we become dissatisfied. Because of this, in the family or at work, there are easily disagreements, even quarrelling.

Therefore, how do you want to program yourself? Do you want to carry your needs and desires around with you and perhaps become a slave to things and circumstances? Or do you want to take your life in hand?

September 19

Take the rudder of your life firmly in hand

Do you have your needs and desires under control? Do you know what you are going to fulfill, so that you can achieve equilibrium in all things and weigh everything carefully, thus becoming increasingly moderate? Then you are no longer the servant of your all-too-human impulses, then you are no longer being controlled or even driven, but hold the rudder of your life firmly in your hand.

September 20

Master the shadows of your days with Christ. He is always with you

Remember: Christ is always with us. He wants to make us happy.
Firmly believe this and you will master the shadows of the days with Christ and be happy and joyful in the evening. Every day brings to everyone the chance to remove from the field of their soul the negativity they planted there. This means that everyone can carry their cross, because Christ carries it with them. If our heart beats for Christ, then the evil will soon be cleared up and overcome.

September 21

By affirming the positive, selfless help grows for your neighbor

If you affirm and find the positive in everything and in everyone, then you are able to give genuine help. Whoever intends and gives real help to others has good hours and a good day. What we give selflessly comes back to us many times over.

September 22

Target the positive for yourself again and again. Then you will increasingly become a seeker of truth

Your new day has announced itself with its thoughts. What thoughts are they? Are they depressing or uplifting? You recognize them yourself. No matter what thoughts move you—always target the positive for yourself, for example, that you want to be just.

If in the morning you target the absolute, such as: "I am just" or: "Justice is at work in me," you will increasingly become a seeker of truth. In time, you will find the truth, the justice, in your thoughts. In your world of thoughts you then experience yourself. If you recognize yourself, you will also know what you should clear up as soon as possible with the power of the Christ of God.

September 23

Your body rhythm shows whether your day is good or less good

You can tell if your day is good or not so good by your body rhythm. If you are calm and joyful, then you have certainly achieved a lot in the positive sense. Thus, you have made your friend, the day, your own, that is, you have made use of it.

If you are unsettled and hectic, know: Even in the hustle and bustle, the day is speaking to you. Clear up what makes you uneasy, then you will become calmer and also partake of your meals thankfully. Do not forget to pray before and after meals. In this way you awaken the feelings of the soul for God, your, our Father.

September 24

Deep gratitude to God makes His power flow

When you are eating your meal, remember that the gifts of love came from God. They grew on the Earth—for you. Many hands have prepared them. Thank God for the gifts, and give thanks for the brothers and sisters who prepared them. Give thanks also after the meal.

In deep thankfulness, which at the same time expresses trust in God, you regain strength for what still needs to be dealt with. Deep thankfulness builds up communication with the power of God; energy flows to you for the further hours of the day.

September 25

Whatever you give comes back to you

If we want to actively shape our life and let develop what lies in it as possibilities, as fullness, then we should often become aware that everything that goes out from us goes back into us.

To bring happiness brings, in turn, happiness. Giving kindness brings, in turn, kindness and understanding. Giving selfless love brings about selfless love. You can be sure: Whatever is positive will also come back to you; it will uplift you and carry you into the days ahead. Your days will then also become brighter, and you will be more joyful.

It is the same with the opposite, the sinful. The sinful is oppressive. The sinful stimulates, in turn, sinfulness. It causes discontent, sadness, despondency and much more. So now you determine your today, your tomorrow, your day after tomorrow—often your future.

September 26

Much can change, if you are willing to change yourself

In our imagination, how often is it the other person who has imposed or forced this or that on us? If this were so, we would also have to once ask ourselves: Why were they able to influence us, where is our weakness here?

Our movement, that is, our agitation, shows that there is something in us as well. We can explore it by looking deeper into our adverse circumstances, asking: Where is my part? What are my feelings toward my neighbors? What do I think about them when I greet them with kind words, for example, or ask them to do this or that for me, etc., etc. It is worthwhile to recognize and find what is not yet in order with us. Many things can change for the better if we are willing to change. Christ helps us do this.

September 27

Today your ego comes toward you again. Recognize the chance therein

Each of us is placed in the new day to clear up, that is, to work through what we once input, whether in this incarnation or in previous incarnations. What has not been cleared up shows up again and again. So in this upcoming day lies a multitude of possibilities, that is, chances, to change some things for the positive.

If disgruntled, angry and similar thoughts still want to determine your day, then go into a brief meditation. Speak your own meditation, and speak it into yourself. Let it come from your feelings. Speak slowly, or think consciously, and accompany your words or your thoughts with your feelings. Then you become calmer; you can accept the day and also fulfill your day's work.

September 28

Overcoming yourself makes you free to do what is right

If we detach ourselves from our shadows, we will find peace in ourselves and the strength to accomplish positively and with strength what is valuable and of service to many.

September 29

What delights you in your inner being helps you, because it inspires you

When you go into the morning prayer, give this your day something to take along: what now delights you in your inner being. It will help you throughout the day, because it will go with you and inspire you.

September 30

Balance, fresh courage and creativity by overcoming what is not good

The day brings you creativity and the solution to many a question. It brings bright spots and pleasant encounters; but it also brings movement, tasks and difficulties that should be reconsidered. If there are unfinished and unpleasant things in your mind, take them to God first, by trying to conclude for yourself what troubles you, that is, what makes you unsettled.

If you want, in a quiet minute sit down in a quiet corner of your apartment or house or perhaps on a park bench. Watch your breath as it comes and goes, so that you can gain distance from your thoughts and view things in the right light, so you can identify the necessary steps and possibly initiate them. Turn trustingly to God, and speak with Him about what moves your disposition. Write down the findings, which you then clear up with your neighbor at the right time.

And do not forget to thank God for His unending help. Thankfulness uplifts the soul and makes for a free heart.

October 1

In every disturbance is a learning task for your day

Could anyone disturb us if what others say were not already latent in us, so that it is awakened by a nudge?

Only our fellow people can disturb us who stimulate associations in us that correspond to the content of their speech. We can say that they then stimulate a correspondence in us.

Why do our thoughts race through our head so massively that we react accordingly, speak quickly and often act hastily and without thinking? If we remain calm within, then we are also balanced without, and the question or the statement of our neighbor cannot disturb us.

This can result in self-recognition and thus, the chance to solve a learning task for the day.

October 2

The true life grows
from within to without

The Kingdom of God can grow out of us only through the refinement of our senses and through thoughts that are willed by God.
In this way, we become reformers of our thoughts and lives, since we are building on the Kingdom of God, which is the true life. The true life grows from within to without; it is the Kingdom of God in us.

Only through spiritualization do we grow closer to God, because God is universal spirit, omnipresent life.

October 3

You are given the strength to change your way of thinking

Are you an optimist or a pessimist, who primarily feels and thinks negatively? We are given the strength to change our way of thinking.

The pessimist might object that it is certainly a long way to go to find a positive view. But that need not be the case. Many of us know how quickly God helps. A positive affirmation that we want to implement and will implement already helps us on the way to healthy optimism.

Just by the fact that we think it possible that we, too, can become happy and be happy, when we believe and affirm that God will help us with this, because He loves us and wants the best for us, our disposition brightens. If we help ourselves attain an upright and joyful attitude by prescribing to ourselves that we want to think positively, that we want to live positively, that we want to be optimistic, that we want to find the good in everything negative, our mood brightens.

This little exercise can brighten your whole day.

October 4

A light heart leads to a cheerful disposition, to openness and understanding

Clear up immediately what is pending, and you will realize that a lighter heart leads to a more cheerful disposition and makes you open to what your neighbors share with you, so that you understand them better.

October 5

Do not poison your inner life and your organism with negative feelings and thoughts

Hatred and all related feelings and thoughts, which include rejection, disparagement, spitefulness and the like, are against the eternal order. With this, we create disorder in our life and also in our body.

If we let thoughts of jealousy, envy, anger or malice and the like run their course, if we thus reinforce them by thinking one and the same thought over and over again, then they poison both our inner life and our organism. These negative energies affect our disposition and manifest themselves again in situations, in events, in blows of fate, in hardships and in worries.

October 6

Be true to yourself!

Your positive attitude toward your day with its situations, events and occurrences is the attitude toward yourself. Thankfulness and contentment and togetherness with your fellow people will be the result.

Why can't you be true to yourself in certain situations? What is going on?

We have become so accustomed to always looking at our neighbor and blaming them. Let's apply our words or our thoughts directed at our neighbor to ourselves and ask ourselves: What is going on with me?

If you become aware of it, you can clear up various components of the day. If you have found peace by clearing up what was pending, then you have also regained an upright and sincere attitude and can say: I am true to myself.

October 7

Settle in the inner kingdom ...

If we want to fulfill our longing for the ideal world, if we want to attain the health of the soul, which can also be transferred to our physical body and if we want to be happy, then we should develop all this in ourselves. The Christ of God, our Redeemer, will help us with this, because it is His concern to make us happy, healthy and joyful, so that we live more and more in the kingdom of the inner being, where true salvation is, our home.

If we want, we can start today to settle in the inner kingdom by becoming positively active in our thoughts and in our behavior. If we keep firmly to this, then our days on Earth will become increasingly filled with light, and our neighbor will then be our heartfelt concern. We give what we ourselves have developed that is positive, as what God wants. Then we are with our fellow people and for them.

October 8

Right thinking and acting bring awareness and unity

If our thinking and acting is good, then our day is fruitful and we are balanced and grateful. If our thinking and acting is predominantly all-too-human, that is, focused on ourselves, on our ego, then we experience that some things prove to be fruitless because where there is no right way of thinking and acting, there is also no deeper recognition, no unity and also no awareness for the next day. As long as we want to work and have an effect only for ourselves, we remain "doers," and our works remain "shoddy efforts." This is then the façade, which is ultimately fruitless and worthless.

What should your daily measure be today—sinful or divine? For example, do you want to be a people-worshipper or a God-worshipper, a "doer" or a good worker? You can explore yourself. Christ will help you.

October 9

An attitude of expectation leads to disappointment and discord

We should not bind ourselves to any person, to any external things such as wealth, power, prestige, or to certain behavior patterns of people. Those who bind themselves put themselves into an attitude of expectation, which always presupposes that we want to get something from others. With our expectation we want to achieve, among other things, a certain equality between us and the people of whom we have expectations. The neighbors are supposed to give us from their energy, and instead we give them from our energy. But since there is nothing that is comparable, because the other can never fulfill our desires according to our expectations, often the expectation turns into disappointment and the disappointment into discord.

October 10

All people bear the core of love, GOD. Do not look only at the faults of your neighbor

Today you will again meet many people. Feel into them. They also come from the cradle of birth of love and bear within the core of love, GOD. Everyone is more or less seeking love. If we do not just look at the faults of our neighbor, but instead feel in them the great kinship, the brotherhood in God, then we can speak much more easily and work together in good communication with the many we meet today.

Be aware of this, and you will experience that your thoughts are far more balanced, calmer and true to life; you will notice that deep joy and inner happiness vivify your heart. This is the answer of the Christ of God to your doing right.

October 11

If you clear up your part, the lake of your disposition will be calmer

During the day, you you are repeatedly moved more strongly, that is, agitated; correspondences are stirred up. However, this should not necessarily be viewed negatively. It is good for you, as long as you are willing to recognize the negative, your part, in the situation, to clear it up and to come into an exchange and positive communication with your neighbor. Thereby, your disposition will grow calmer again; the lake of your disposition will be calmer, so that you will be able to again hear the voice of your day.

October 12

Overcome the annoyance over your neighbor

In the end, our fellow people are always the cause of our anger, our resentment, our dissatisfactions, our ire. But are they therefore also the guilty ones?

Perhaps the following words will help you to overcome your annoyance over your neighbor:
Those who affirm the good in their neighbor awaken it in themselves. This is then their life as well.
Dear brother, dear sister, each of us wants to be happy. But happiness enters our heart only when we welcome our neighbor into our heart.

October 13

Do not look to others— become independent within

Those who keep themselves more and more away from the multitude in order to recognize God's will, which sets in motion what is good and positive in a person, will become increasingly independent inwardly. They no longer look to others, but act according to their inner knowledge.

Thus, they gradually become wise. They are turned toward God and not toward the multitude. Although they are often among the multitude, they are nevertheless not seen, because they are not courted by it and do not court it. They do not cultivate communication with the many never-satisfied egos, of which "the multitude" consists.

Ask yourself: What do I want? Do I want to present myself to the multitude to be seen, to be in the middle, so as to get the stale all-too-human energy? Or do I set out to ask for God's will and to fulfill it?

October 14

Overcome the base self—become peaceful, because you hear the voice of the present, your true self

Already early in the morning, we hear ourselves. Do we hear the base self, our sinful inputs—or do we hear the higher self, our divine heritage? We ourselves have determined this and determine it every day anew.

If we move our sinful thoughts, then we multiply the negative energy and continue to store this accordingly in our conscious mind and subconscious, in our soul, in the heavenly bodies and in the atmosphere. These inputs of today will again become the voice of a day for us in the future. However, if we are alert, if it is all our thoughts and energy to grow closer to God again, then with the help of the Christ of God in us, we will clear up as quickly as possible the sinfulness that we recognize, to no longer think the same and like things.

Then we will be less and less unsettled, aggressive, envious and quarrelsome, and instead, more and more peaceful, because we hear the voice of the present, our divine heritage, our true self.

October 15

A full subconscious causes disharmony

If we are fairly balanced, then we are also in harmony, and our day will proceed more consciously, because we are living *in* the day, which implies that our feelings and thoughts, that is, our consciousness, are with us.

If we are divided, if we dwell on unfinished and unpleasant things, then even what normally gives us relaxation, respite and pleasure will hardly bring us joy, because our subconscious is filled with what still preoccupies us. We find ourselves in disharmony; our feelings and thoughts are one time here, then again there. Then we are outside of ourselves with our consciousness, and the result is that we lose mental and physical strength. Because of this, joy and initiative also dwindle.

How can you gain inner harmony?

Face the disharmony in your world of feelings and thoughts and ask yourself if you want it to stay that way. Then—if you want to—change yourself!

October 16

Unburden your conscious mind and your subconscious, so that during the night your soul is able to draw strength in higher regions of light

*E*very day brings the chance that we unburden our conscious mind and our subconscious and thus create space in our soul for the positive power. Then in the evening there is rest for the soul and the person.

Therefore, we should free our conscious mind and our subconscious from ballast, by clearing up what moves us.

The fewer current issues vibrate in the conscious mind and the subconscious, the deeper you sleep. Through deep sleep, you enable your soul to go to lighter regions of the universe, and, according to its state of consciousness, to receive light energies, high life forces.

October 17

The inner wealth opens up in the one who becomes modest. Achieve inner greatness

The divine law says: The more modest people become, the more their inner wealth opens up. Only then do they truly give meaning to their lives and attain the inner greatness that stands above trifles and pressing desires.

Dear brother, dear sister, you determine yourself how you want to be. Now is a new day. You go into this day. How? You determine that yourself.

October 18

What could my day possibly bring? Let yourself be prepared by your soul

In order to live more and more in the presence of God, we should analyze the unresolved aspects of past days on Earth, our past, that is, what preoccupies and moves us from past life situations, what does not allow our thoughts to come to rest. Only when we clear up our burdened past and no longer push back into the past, into the realm of our shadows, what the day reveals to us in terms of sinfulness, but instead set ourselves the task of overcoming it, will we gradually become quieter, and sense already in the morning some impulses from the subconscious for the dawning day. If you are given a few minutes of peace in the morning, you can practice this.

We do not have to go blindly into the day with the anxious question of what it may bring. Let your soul prepare you through your subconscious and then via the more concretely tangible, the conscious mind.

October 19

Behind the clouds the sun is shining. Do you accept it?

We have the habit of brooding for a long time over evils such as grievances, fear, suffering and failures. This makes us listless, grumpy and sad.

Let us remember: Behind the clouds the sun is shining! And let us be aware: God, the inner sun, is much brighter, more luminous and radiant! It stands above our listlessness, above our grumpiness and our sadness. It never turns away from us.

How will you deal with today? Know that God, who is behind every sadness, behind every state of dejection, always shines His light of love and peace to you.

October 20

Plan consciously with God, and live consciously with Him

A day lies before you. Your day consists of what you previously input. Do you want to meet the situations of your day?

If you can maintain a positive attitude toward the day, then the end of the day will also be an inner celebration, a thankfulness to God who guided you through your day.

Surely you have resolved to keep to the good planning on this day. In the evening, if you want, briefly review your plan for tomorrow and place that plan in God's hands.

God is active for you, also in the night.

October 21

Leave your neighbors the freedom to take their learning steps

Nobody can solve our problems for us. However, we are alone, completely on our own, only when we solely expect to get something that is comparable to our ideas. The spiritual development and further development of humankind lies in togetherness, in that everyone lives their daily rhythm, the content of their day.

From our personal experiences we can help our neighbor, provided we have mastered the same or like things, which, however, are not identical to what they have to master. Thus, we can never force our experiences on anyone else, but merely provide assistance on the basis of what we have overcome.

For this reason, we should support our neighbor with advice and help only if they want this, but never influence them, because those who have to recognize and resolve their affairs can carry out their valuable learning steps from this.

Therefore take a step back, and let your neighbor have their learning process. This is a divine law that leads to freedom and understanding love.

October 22

> You determine the engraving in your soul and on your body. Let Christ help you to develop the good!

Every day, we are the forger of our well-being or discomfort, of our moods and inhibitions. The anvil is our ego, on which our body lies. The blacksmith is our will, which engraves the manifestation, the expression of our thoughts on our face and determines our posture.

We ourselves decide each day and every moment about our earthly existence. We determine the engraving in our soul, in and on our body.

Christ wants to help us develop the good, the noble and the ethical. Let's allow ourselves to be helped and call upon Him, then we will, if possible, immediately clear up with Him what is still in disorder. But in a quiet hour we will also thank Him for what we have already put in order and for what we will put in order with His help, in order to attain inner confidence so that He can work through us.

October 23

Awaken the positive powers in you!

If you can begin the day in a balanced and harmonious rhythm, then your feelings and thoughts are according to this. If you take the time for deep prayer, you will experience that powers are latent in you that knock on your heart and that want to be awakened by you.

Thus, if you want, go into a deep morning prayer and experience the positive powers in you. Indeed, experience your innermost being in prayer. It reveals itself in the most subtle feelings, in the most subtle nuances of thought.

If during the day you find yourself thinking about your fellow people, ask yourself what kind of thoughts you are having. If they do not correspond to the order from which peace and harmony flow, then think about the following: It is the positive forces that are waiting to be awakened, so as to be able to work through us.

October 24

Be honest with yourself!

Would you like to take into your awareness some words that Christ, our Redeemer and Friend, gave us in His great cosmic teachings?
"Therefore examine whether what you want to do corresponds to your innermost being and serves your spiritual growth. So be honest with yourselves. Do nothing that is contrary to the eternal truth, to the eternal Being, because nothing is hidden from God. What you have concealed will be revealed one day, and you will see whether your thinking and acting was upright and honest."

October 25

God loves you.
He helps and He serves you.
How do you want to be with Him?

Realize again and again: God, our Father in Christ, helps you and each of us at every moment, because He is always in us and thus, always with us. He wants us to be happy, because He is happiness. He wants us to be peaceful and joyful, because He is peace and joy.

God loves each one of us. He helps you; He helps all of us. He serves you; He serves all of us. He wants the best for you and for all of us, because He is our Father.

How do you want to be with Him?

October 26

Through a positive alignment and acceptance of the day, you achieve inner freedom

When you sigh and say, "Oh dear, the daily routine again, again the bonds of work," know that your inner being is unfree.

If you recognize this in the morning and free yourself of it already in the morning, by aligning yourself positively and consciously accepting the day, then many a shackle will fall away. Maybe there is something wrong in your family that troubles your mind? Perhaps there are disagreements with your boss, with your colleagues or with your friends? You know it yourself; the morning has already spoken to you. Because what you move in your thoughts or in your feelings are signs of a lack of freedom, signs of what needs to be cleared up, so that you can gain inner freedom and begin your day's work with the power of Christ.

October 27

You encounter yourself in your neighbor

You experience yourself again and again. How did you encounter yourself? That is also how you encountered your neighbor. Spoken the other way around: The way you encountered your neighbor, that is how you encountered yourself. You have now again input this into the rhythms of the day and what you have input, positive or negative, lawful or unlawful, comes toward you again. Therefore, it is good if you clear up what is negative right away. Then this will no longer determine your future days. So if some things still need to be cleared up, do it, if you want to.
And be aware: God helps.

October 28

Practice being in communication with the forces of creation

Practice being in communication with the forces of creation, the elements, and very soon you will realize that the elements serve you.

You will feel that the sun tells you when to go into the shade, that the clouds communicate and tell you to take rain gear with you when you go hiking today. The Earth tells you how you should walk, that you should pay attention to animals and plants. And the air, whether it is cool or warm, chimes in and tells you that the Spirit of the heavenly Creator God is flowing in it as well, touching you.

October 29

Do not wait until tomorrow!

Day after day, it is a matter of recognizing and removing the little plants of our unkindness that we have sown or are sowing in thoughts, words and deeds, before we have to reap the fruit of our sin. Still today, we should recognize what we have sown today or previously. What was sown today is still in our conscious mind, and we grasp it more quickly. Moreover, the new seed is not yet in the soul.

So do not wait until tomorrow. After your day's work, look back on your day before you go to your family or friends and acquaintances. Tune into being calm and attune yourself to it. If possible, what needs to be cleared up, that is, what depresses you and makes you restive, nullify it in the evening with the help of the Christ of God in you. And when you have cleared up what is depressing you close the day with Christ. Do not forget to give thanks for everything.

October 30

Become a good conversation partner

By clearing things up, we offset the imbalance of our disposition. The balance of our disposition gives us security and degrees of inwardness. We are then also good and conscious conversation partners who do not simply speak out whatever comes to mind. We consider and express only what we can also advocate in our thoughts. That gives strength and awareness.

October 31

With the help of the Inner Light, penetrate the negativity and find the positive in it

If your day brings not only joyful things, but also situations that cause the barometer of your mood to fall, then say to yourself, for example: "I am an optimist. The positive power is in everything. Even in the gloomy, in the dark, in every veiled situation, the positive power is there, which I affirm. Thus, with the help of the Inner Light, I shine through the negative and find the positive in it."

If you keep falling into pessimism, you eventually let yourself fall into self-pity, gloom and resignation, and then your body becomes heavier because your feelings and thoughts come into a lower vibration. If you can hold onto optimism or build it up again by actively affirming the positive force, then you will see how your body gets lighter and more buoyant, because your thoughts are brighter and lighter.

How do you want to do it today? We can note down the good intentions, guidelines for the coming hours of the day, so that we can refer back to them during the course of the day. This gives a sense of security and makes us feel confident.

November 1

Faults, weaknesses, difficulties— impulses for rethinking, for change

The situations that the day brings us and what we perceive with our senses that irritates us also has within the energy, that is, the strength, for us to recognize ourselves, to clear up what is sinful and to stop doing it.

Consequently, each day is a gift. No matter what it brings us—it merely brings us back to ourselves. This is not always pleasant. Our faults and weaknesses often get us into difficulties. This is how the learning tasks in the school of life called Earth show themselves. They are impulses for rethinking, for change.

November 2

Today you can become a little bit freer, more cheerful and happy

*E*ach day has many moments that have many a thing to tell you.
This day is also your day. Today it brings you what you can recognize and clear up today. If you are alert, you will discover yourself, because the day speaks to us from countless mouths. Today you can again lighten your soul and conscience and become a little freer, more cheerful and happy.

November 3

You determine how the strings of your life sound

You know you have free will. How you tune into your life is how your life is.

You determine how the strings of your life sound. They consist of your feelings, sensations, thoughts, words and actions. Perhaps you will think about this. Then you will surely find it easier to clear up some things with Christ and to no longer do them.

November 4

I want God, my Father, to be pleased with me

*S*ome words for you to think about: What does being in God mean to you? Do you want to know what it means to me? It means to me that I don't want to be here or there. Nor am I drawn to be here or there; I do not want to be attached to any earthly place because the place of rest, the eternal home, is within me. Therefore, for me, my home is neither on Earth nor anywhere else, not even on this or that planet; I am not attracted there either.

I want neither praise nor acknowledgment, but solely that God, My Father, is pleased with me. I strive neither for rank nor prestige; I want to only be His child. That is my present thinking. And that is how I act in every situation.

Dear brother, dear sister, you now know how I do it. You decide yourself how you want to do it.

November 5

Find the good in and on you and in your surroundings …

There is joy in the good.
There is also much good for you today. Do not look for the bad; find the good in and on you and in your surroundings and be glad in it. Then you will not only look at yourself, at your all-too-human aspects, but will gain foresight and insight into the situations of the day.

November 6

Turn fully to your neighbor and the situation—live consciously!

We often have expectations of our neighbor instead of meeting them halfway, or we have expectations of what the day should bring us, instead of letting God act and prevail. That causes disappointment; we are off balance.

If we turn fully and consciously to our neighbor in a situation, we can grasp the message of our neighbor and of the situation. But often our thoughts revolve around ourselves. Then we may well have heard some of what our neighbor said, but it was a mechanical, superficial hearing. Basically, we could not really understand the whole thing. Often, this makes us uneasy. To briefly clear up what the day brings in the way of unpleasantness, of doubtfulness, helps us to be prudent and calm and to live consciously.

November 7

Read where you stand on your barometer

If we want to push through our desires, our opinions and ideas, then, as the words "push through" express, we feel pressure in the stomach area. *We* want to talk; *we* want to clarify the situation; *we* think we know better. As a result, we become agitated, hectic, tense, and thus, stressed.

Our state of mind, our world of thoughts and our body rhythm show us how our day is going. We ourselves are the barometer. Read where you stand on your barometer. Are you balanced? Are you hectic? Are you under stress? Everything wants to tell you something.

You yourself, your feelings and thoughts, are the scale. Which thoughts are weighty? For example, which people do you measure with the scale of your thoughts? That is, what do you think about them?

Check the weight of your thoughts and apply the standard of true Christian ethics and morals to your thinking. Then you will know what you should clear up in and on yourself. If you do this with Christ's help, you will become balanced. Then the day will be a conscious day, because you take your balance, that is, your harmony, into the day.

November 8

What you do not change today is already the past tomorrow

The now and today, the moment, is given to us to act and to have an effect. What we do not change today will already be the past tomorrow.
Let us more often be aware of *what* the day that is passing will take with it into our past. Does it really take along the past, that is, what we have completed and finished? Then no shadow remains in us, but memories, aspects of our own true life experience. Or does a part of our exceedingly human thoughts, words and actions, what we have not cleared up and remedied today, go into the past to come back at some time or other and determine our future?
Today is still today; you can still act. Make use of today.

November 9

Think positively!
Practice makes perfect

Surely today will bring many a good and positive thing for you—namely, if you look for and find the good and positive in the situations and in your fellow people. Even if you don't always succeed, try it once more!

Try again and again. To think negatively is often like an ingrained program. We have to make several attempts to change it. But here, too, practice makes perfect.

November 10

Change your thinking! Then higher thoughts come into your life, which open you for the fullness of God

All doubting, nagging, hateful and quarrelsome thoughts poison us and lead us into sickness, hardship and poverty.

Therefore, we should be alert and recognize all these thoughts with the help of the Christ of God. We should repent, clear them up and stop thinking like that. The moment we start to clear them up and resolve for divine principles of the law, we will talk less and less about illness, hardship, suffering, poverty and the like. We will become aware of the attraction of positive forces and send out positive, that is, lawful thoughts and words. Then we will receive more and more from the fullness of God, health, strength, help, inner wealth, food, clothing, shelter and much more.

However, everything first has to be worked out by us, by changing how we think in the situations of the day. If we recognize our sinfulness, which the day shows us in portions, if we clear it up with the help of the Christ of God and no longer cultivate these thoughts, higher thoughts will enter our life: thoughts of peace, thoughts of hope, thoughts of strength, thoughts of being one with God. In this way, we open ourselves to the inflow of the fullness of God, and we will receive from the fullness what we need as children of God, and many times beyond this.

November 11

Affirm God, the light, in all things, and you will go through your life on Earth more serenely, confidently and cheerfully

*I*f you turn to the inner sun and draw from it energy, hope and vigor, then you are cheerful and in a joyful mood, because your day's work is fulfilled; you fill the day and your work with life; you think and ultimately, attribute to yourself the strength and the life from God.

Do not give up affirming the good that God is in all things, and that He is above all sorrow, above all worries, above illness and hardship and suffering! Affirm God, the light, the warm sun, in all things, and you will go through your life on Earth more serene and sunnier from within, that is, more confident and cheerful.

November 12

Music creates a different vibration and thus, different feelings and thoughts. Become an explorer of your life

Music creates a different rhythm, a different vibration for your body and for your disposition, and thus, different feelings and thoughts. They, too, reveal your traits, your character to you.

Become an explorer of your life and you explore your own inputs from the past hours of your years. Only in this way, can you master your life and take your fate into your own hands.

November 13

Undo the violation of the law and become free

Don't say that there is so much to overcome. If there are still countless violations of the law, don't let a feeling of resignation come up! Ask God to give you many more days, so that you can clear up parts of your transgressions each day, the corteges of fate are voided and you become a person who lives consciously, who always weighs things: when wanting to blurt out something; when tormented by thoughts; when thoughts of anger, hatred and envy well up.

Consider: What do you want? To live happily and freely, or to experience your inputs, your blows of fate?

Every violation of the law has consequences. If you undo them, you enter the law of love, of forgiveness, of understanding, and you are free of your ego.

November 14

Why humble yourself to be, for once, "the greatest"?

Do you want to let the carousel of thoughts revolve in you today, that you want to be in the center and swim in the sea of the masses of people, in the waves of the many egos? Or do you want to devote yourself to Christ again and again, so that Christ can be the center of your thinking, feeling and wanting? Then perhaps your inner eyes will open so that you can realize how many of our neighbors present themselves to the masses, to receive recognition, applause and more all-too-human energy, as many a one uses their elbows to swim along with the masses. Perhaps you can recognize in the situations of the day what it is like when you or others of the masses bow down, and can increasingly see through why you or others humble themselves, in order to finally be, for once, the greatest.

November 15

Unlock the treasures of your heart

If we immediately remedy what makes us uneasy, our subconscious becomes calmer and more balanced. Then the treasures of our heart, the again opened aspects of our eternal heritage, come into play more and more.

If we cannot clear up what is troubling us, perhaps because our neighbor does not want to speak to us, during our morning prayer we should surrender this matter to Christ and firmly resolve not to let out of our heart the good that is in every person.

However, we should no longer do our part of what led to disharmony between our neighbor and ourselves. If we always strive for being in balance with our fellow people, then the Christ of God will also help us.

Look into your heart! You have in hand what vibrates in your heart. We should put in order what moves negatively in our conscious mind and subconscious, so that we are with ourselves, that is, *in* the day.

November 16

What is still unpleasant does not have to stay that way

We achieve harmony by concentrating on our activity and by planning our work well. Of course, we can achieve the goal of our planning only if we include our fellow people, who are our neighbors, if we are *with* them and *for* them. This results in a good communication, which makes the positive, the helping forces flow. We are also able to concentrate only when we are for and with our fellow people.

If you are not really satisfied with your day, ask yourself what is not in order with you. With whom were you or are you at odds? If your work is difficult for you—where are your thoughts? Or do you dislike the work? And if so, why is this so? Clear up what you recognize and set a new course. Christ, the Helper in you, gives you His strength.

November 17

Strive for cosmic thinking. It's worth it!

Strive for self-reflection, and you will be in the day and with the day. When in the evening the day leaves you, then you will also give it good works to take along. These works are *your* works. They come back to you in the rhythm of your days.

No matter what the day brings to you, strive for cosmic thinking! It's worth it!

Stay alert and accept the good friend, the day, and all that it brings you.

November 18

If you take one step toward God, He will take several steps toward you

If you don't always succeed in what you set out to do today, do not be sad—God is always with you. Try again; even a conscious, earnest effort is a step toward God. If we take one step toward God with an honest heart, He will come several steps toward us.

November 19

Learn to master your thoughts and to concentrate

We are on this Earth to learn. In the school on Earth, we also learn to recognize ourselves. We recognize what we think and how we feel.

Those who gradually recognize themselves no longer apply a standard to their neighbor, but to themselves and are stricter with themselves; they do not let themselves get away with everything. They make an effort to know their thoughts, to master them, in order to be able to focus, that is, to concentrate.

If you do not always succeed in keeping your thoughts in check, then you know where your weak points are. Go to the center. Christ helps you to recognize your weaknesses, to find the root, to clear it up and to no longer do it.

November 20

See yourself and your neighbor as a son, a daughter of God; gain respect, understanding, tolerance and good will

If you grow into the awareness "God helps me; He is always for me and with me; He is always present," you will learn to see yourself as a son, a daughter of God. Then you will better understand your fellow people, and very gradually you will gain respect for God in them. From the respect for God in your neighbor, understanding, tolerance and good will awaken.

However, you do not have to say yes to everything and approve of something bad. Those who have respect for God in their neighbor appreciate them; they are with them and for them. This results in a positive communication and with this, surely a good conversation in which you can address what is not in order.

November 21

Reduce the many words. With self-discipline you use the time and gain new and deeper insights and recognitions

Following, a help for your day: Reduce the many words. Consider whether what you want to say now is useful for you and for your neighbor. And reduce the flood of thoughts by calling on Christ again and again, asking Him for help. You will soon realize that you become calmer and gain more time for the work at hand.

Through this self-discipline you will experience that you make better use of the time and that you always gain new and deeper recognitions and insights.

November 22

Now and today you set the course for further positive days

Is your day good? Many a person will say, "Mixed. It has the most disparate moods." Who doesn't feel that way? Each of us is on our way into the light and is not yet perfect light. Each day, areas of our shadows catch up with us again until we have transformed them into light with the power of the Christ of God.

Therefore, if we accept our cross, our burdens, to recognize ourselves in them and, with the help of Christ, to clear up the recognized faults and no longer do them, the days will become more light-filled and brighter.

If you keep this up, you will set the course for more positive days.

November 23

The work on yourself leads to a conscious life

Self-exploration through self-observation allows us to see some things that could be changed. But we have free will.
To recognize ourselves, then decide whether to leave it at that or to clear it up and change it, and then to also do it—that is the work on ourselves. This work on ourselves is an essential part of our existence on Earth, because only then will we live consciously and master life more and more.

November 24

The awareness of being part of the great Creator-power brings distance from worries and difficulties

The day is determined, among other things, by the elemental forces, because flowers, shrubs, trees, all plants and all animals are one with the elements, with fire, the same as light, with water, with soil and air. The elements serve nature, and nature is oriented to the elements.

What do we orient ourselves to? If we orient ourselves to God by fulfilling God's commandments step by step, then we will be for the elements more and more and will be with them, so that they also serve us accordingly.

Nature gives itself. Give yourself to the air, to feel in your deep and conscious breath the life that wants to refresh, strengthen and fill you.

If we become aware that we are partakers of the great Creator-power, the thoughts of loneliness leave us and we gain distance from worries and difficulties, from our all-too-human aspects. The power of God is active in the elemental forces.

November 25

Rid yourself of wants and desires to let the inner richness fill you

Perhaps the following words from the divine Wisdom can say something to you:
"What we want we do not possess, and what we humanly have does not belong to us. We must rid ourselves of all wanting and desiring and let the inner wealth fill us. Then we will never be externally in want either."

November 26

Inner balance leads to conscious acting. This results in joy and a positive result for the day

A meditative prayer in the morning hours brings you balance and a harmonious attitude toward your work. The balance of the heart also brings increased joy in the small, nice things of everyday life, namely, in what you do joyfully.
Perhaps today there is time for a run in the woods, a walk, a training hour for the body, gardening? Even if you pursue your hobby—with inner balance it is done consciously. This brings joy and surely leads to a positive result for the day.

November 27

Do not join the masses to strive for recognition. Build up inner strength

Be aware: The masses do not recognize you. Everyone in the masses just want to be recognized only by themselves. But God knows you, His child.

Clear up the pressing things. Realize that your disposition will be more spiritually elevated when you feel what it means not to go into the masses to strive for recognition. In this way, you will develop more and more inner strength, from which you will be able to give selflessly.

Those who give selflessly receive. They receive from the eternal source, God, the life. They will find their way externally to those who do not pay homage to the majority of people, to the ego of many, to the striving for recognition and the pursuit of human energy. They find their way to those who give honor to God in their lives and can look back on the fulfilled works of the day.

November 28

Explore and clear up your base self and find your way to the higher Self

Be aware that thoughts and words are symbols. Recognize yourself in the symbols. Experience your traits, your character.

We explore our base self in our words, in our thoughts.

All our glances, that is, our "glimpses" or what we hear wants to tell us something. Whatever especially moves us is part of our daily task today. What we saw, what we heard, speaks to us.

If we learn the symbolic language today, we recognize ourselves better and better. Those who do not want to recognize themselves remain trapped in their own fallacy and believe that their way of thinking and behaving is the be-all and end-all.

November 29

Like you, your neighbor is loved by God

God loves you; God loves me—God loves all of us.

No matter how your neighbor may approach you, like you, he is loved by God. If you realize this, his human weaknesses will no longer seem so serious to you.

November 30

Let the voice of the day speak to you

Your inputs are the voice of your day. Your day speaks to you in your feelings, sensations and thoughts and in the movements of your disposition.

Your day's work is well done when you listen to what the voice of the day tells you. Do not immediately oppose the voice of the day with ifs and buts, the all-too-human excuses, but let the moments, the situations, speak to you in your emotions. Your disposition is the scale on which you can read what is less good or what is good, that is, what has already been remedied and what needs to be cleared up.

Remember: In each one of us is the Helper and Guide, Christ. In the voice of the day is the help, Christ. Let Him be active, and you will live more consciously. Either you live and deal with the present or you prepare the situations for the future.

December 1

Stay collected, and draw closer to the Inner Light

If our thoughts and feelings have gone astray during a conversation, we do not fill our words with truthfulness. This makes us uneasy.

If we succeed in primarily expressing the essentials, then we realize how helpful this is. We become calmer and can also work more concentrated. If we become quieter, we remain collected and consciously stay with ourselves. We become more and more aware of our inner self, which is divine. Through this we come closer to the Inner Light that wants to shine and work through us.

December 2

You and I are children from God's cradle of love

The light of the day is God. God is light. God is love. You and I, all human beings, are children of God, children from God's cradle of love, born from His holy law.

Many people have turned away from the cradle of love, the birthplace of their true existence. They do not know that God is love, that God is the Father of all people. To experience that God is love, we must learn the commandment of love for God and neighbor again; for only those who love God know that God loves them. Those who do not love God have turned away from God and love the world.

Whenever unloving and disparaging thoughts come again, realize: They do not belong in the cradle of our birth; they do not belong to the eternal law of love, to our divine heritage.

December 3

Where there are shadows, there is also light

If you know your day, you know a part of yourself. Do not say that there are many shadows. Know that if there are shadows, there must also be light. If you are willing to clear up the shadows you recognize, then the sun will shine. The sun dynamizes you, gives you strength and inner joy. If you then eat your meal, you will realize that the gifts of nature also delight you, because you consciously partake of them.

Remember: In everything and in everyone is God. Thus, no sinner needs to despair.

December 4

Truth or illusion—
for or against God?

If you decide for the truth, you have chosen well, namely the good, the divine. You have not chosen the comfortable, because if you are serious, then you will have to decide again and again each day: Truth—or illusion, that is, appearance? This means: for or against God?

How will you decide? It is entirely up to you, because you have, like all of us, free will.

December 5

The power of God is also in the negative

God is always there for you and wants the best for you. He loves you. He radiates to you in all that comes to you. He also speaks to you in suffering and gives you the strength to overcome it. If you are aware of this, you will certainly raise your heart to God to give heartfelt thanks for everything that you have encountered, for joy and for sorrow. Once you have overcome the suffering, you can say: Neither worry nor suffering bring me to my knees, because I know I am in God.

DECEMBER 6

Your life plan— a plan of faithfulness

A good life plan that corresponds to the truth, the law of God, is a plan of faithfulness, namely, to remain faithful to the One to whom you have promised: Christ, the truth. At the same time, you also remain faithful to yourself, namely, to your true self, which is divine. Each day, you must overcome yourself to remain faithful to your plan of faithfulness. Overcoming oneself involves not only courage, but being alert to recognize the deceptive, seductive thoughts and to clear them up with Christ. However, if you are aware that God is love, that God is your Father, the Father of us all, then it goes much better.

December 7

By joyfully affirming the good in the day, you will make the best of everything

Out of the positive from God come dynamism and freshness—a vitality that makes life worth living, that is *for* the neighbor and that, in turn, affirms the positive in everything we encounter, developing in our world of thoughts and senses. If you go into the day by joyfully affirming the good, then you will make the best of everything. Often you will encounter what you radiate: friendliness, understanding, good will.

December 8

Opinions of people or the will of God— what is valid for you?

What should be valid for you in the hours of your day—the opinions of people or God's will?

We cannot just push away the opinions of our neighbors and say, "They don't interest me." One thing we can do, however: We can deduce from our neighbors' opinions a spiritual principle of God's law. And if we affirm this, we can also go to our neighbors with this principle, so that we do not reject their opinion and concept, but bring in what may also help them.

During the day, frequently become aware that "no" separates us from our neighbor. The solution creates access to our neighbor.

December 9

Unfold the fullness from God in you

External wealth makes no impression on me. For me, to be rich means to possess God's wisdom. I do not think of deprivation, because I bear in me the most beautiful pearls of life: the heavens. This is the height to climb in order to live in God.

Dear brother, dear sister, the fullness from God is in you. Do you want to unfold it? You decide yourself what you want to do about it.

December 10

Be a bringer of happiness!

So be a bringer of happiness, then the happiness of others will also bring you happiness. Many moments of the day give you the opportunity. As long as we look only at the faults of others, we always look only at our own faults. As long as we get upset at the faults of others, we get upset at our own faults. As long as we disparage others, we belittle ourselves.

Thus, everything we think about others, we think toward ourselves. We input this into our memory bank, into the subconscious and the conscious mind, into the soul and into the heavenly bodies —and this comes back to us.

If we make an effort each day to understand our neighbors, if we give them a little help so that they may become happy or remain happy, then we will also find our own happiness. It is the happiness that lasts: the inner happiness, the connection with God, our Father.

December 11

Today is the day!

What did your soul bring along into the day?
It speaks through your feelings, through your thoughts.
Think briefly about what your soul told you in the morning when you woke up. You will surely analyze the disharmonies and know that some unresolved things are pending: past conversations, situations and things that should have been cleared up long ago.
Today is the day that brings the chance to clear these up, so that your soul become free and your person feel deep, inner joy. Then you will also bring joy to those around you. For the joy that comes from the heart also enters the heart of your fellow people.

December 12

Learn from mistakes

Even if the hours rush by, the day is sure to bring some things with it—joy, but also irritation and sorrow.

Resolve to always go to the center, to Christ. Even if you say that you have not always been able to do it, for example, that you have been at odds with your neighbor in a situation, or that you have had disagreements at work, know that none of us is perfect.

We learn from our mistakes, but also from the mistakes of our neighbors; for if we see a shortcoming in our neighbor and do not disparage our neighbor, then we know that *we* should not do the same or similar thing.

December 13

Your future and thus your fate are in your hands

Each day holds a secret, as it were, which it reveals situation by situation, minute by minute, moment by moment. This secret, whose content reveals itself in the moments of our day, becomes tangible for us in our life on Earth, in our experience, in our fate. It is our day; it is our existence, our fate—and the secret is also our secret.

Our life on Earth consists of days. Each day brings us again what we have given to the days in the past. The days bring again what has become the past and was not cleared up by us. We then call that the future.

Your future, and thus your fate, is in your hands.

December 14

Live consciously, so that it is a fulfilled day

If today some things do not go as you imagined and you are uneasy in this respect, perhaps hectic or even depressed, then check your thoughts. They tell you what you can clear up.

If you always create balance in yourself, then you will also establish an inner connection with your co-workers, with your family members, with your friends, and the relationship with your neighbors will be a good one.

Meet them as a conscious son, a conscious daughter of God, as a brother or sister among brothers and sisters. And know: God loves all of us equally.

December 15

In movement is the strength for change

You say that today is a day filled with movement? Movement is good, dear brother, dear sister, because in movement is the strength for change. Whether this change is for the better or for the worse, you alone decide. Therefore, the message to you today is: "Everything can change for the better if I change it in me for the better."

December 16

To be happy means to make your neighbor happy

The happiness we strive for depends on us, on the way we feel, think, speak and act. To be happy means to make your neighbor happy—not with many gifts, but with sincere, God-filled thoughts, words, gestures or actions.

Clear up in your thoughts what needs to be cleared up. Then you will be free and happy in your heart. From a happy heart flows a happy prayer of thanks, which then also grants you a happy day.

December 17

No shadow remains forever

The light of the day brings you your life—many, many moments in which you encounter many things, primarily yourself.

The light of day shows you the bright side of your life and also the dark sides. But do not be afraid. The shadows have no power over you if you look at them with courage and clear them up. Christ helps you do this. His power, the Redeemer-power, the Redeemer-light, is in you and transforms the shadows.

No shadow remains forever! All of us, you and I and all our brothers and sisters, are children of the light who one day will long for the light and strive for the light. Each of us is on Earth to transform our shadows, our sins, into light with Christ, our Redeemer.

December 18

The key to the kingdom of heaven is in you

There are days of reflection, days of rest, but it is good to always be level-headed during the day. Reflect on the good and realize that each day is a gift from the Eternal, given to us so that we may recognize our human aspects, clear them up and no longer do them.

Know that God is in you and you are the temple of God. If you like, think about this. Many seek the key to the kingdom of heaven here and there and yet, do not find it. The key to the kingdom of heaven is in the heart of each one alone. The key is Christ; He is the key to the door of life.
He is in you.

December 19

The feelings that accompany your words tell you what is between you and your neighbor

What's the point of a conversation if you don't know the meaning of what you or the other person is saying? Frequently, we have to use so many words because we often think we are not understood. "He doesn't understand me"—but the other is not understood by you either!

Solely through the language of the heart, can we learn to understand one another. If both parties were well-disposed toward one another, if each was devoted to the other from the heart, then they would be heartfelt brothers and sisters from the Spirit of God and their hearts would be in accord with one another and with our Father in heaven, who is the might and power of the All. Then our feelings, sensations and thoughts would be divine and our words would radiate their content: the language of the heart. Then there would be fewer quarrels and disagreements; there would be no long conversations with "ifs and buts" or "maybes." There would be clarity in our words because we have clarified everything with one another and are thus one in the unity of God, one with His heart, with the law of love for God and neighbor.

December 20

Lasting happiness comes solely from within

No one can make another person happy in the long run, because lasting happiness comes only from within.
But we can make a person happy through a selfless gift, a small gift, a loving gesture for which we ask nothing, not even a thank you.

December 21

Make use of the power of your Redeemer, Christ. Bring a gem from the treasure of the inner being to shine

You can recognize yourself if you pay attention to your conscience, which shows you via your feelings whether you have spoken or acted correctly or unlawfully. We know the uneasy feeling in the stomach area that shows us that something is out of order in us—but also the free and joyful feeling that signals us that we have resolved some things lawfully, that is, according to the Ten Commandments of God.

Each of the many moments of the day brings you the energy and help to recognize yourself, and the opportunity to bring a small or larger gem from the treasure of the inner being to shine—if in each situation, you connect with Christ, the Inner Helper and Advisor, and make use of His strength.

December 22

Let the day become your good friend!

Let the day become your good friend! It speaks to you and points out to you what you should clear up today and thus, change, but also what you have already cleared up. That is the light-filled sides of your life, the joy and harmonious. If the day perhaps brings you sorrow, perhaps also despondency—in everything you can recognize yourself, so that you can find your way to your true self.

December 23

You are not alone. Christ's strength is in you

You do not go through the day alone, nor are you now totally on your own.
Christ is present.
Christ in you—that is the most important thing.
Christ is the Helper and Advisor in us.
After an honest reflection, in which you clear up some things, you will very soon realize that peace draws into your disposition. We have often experienced it: The heart becomes lighter; our thoughts are more positive. We feel the strength of Christ in us. In the harmonious, peaceful and uplifting power, go to your neighbor and into the rest of the day.

December 24

Attain the melodiousness of your soul; fulfill the will of the heavenly Father

Pause and listen to the sound of your soul. The melodiousness of our soul tells us that we were and are in unity with our neighbor. The melodiousness of our soul tells us that we have given thanks more than we have demanded; that we have stepped back where we could have required; that we have given more than we have taken; that we have arbitrated instead of giving orders; that we have reconciled instead of punishing in thought and word.

If we fulfill the will of our heavenly Father in this or like ways, then we will also think of Him more often, because thankfulness stirs in our heart and we feel His nearness.

December 25

To honor God in all things is to be a true Christian

If you hold the spiritual palm of peace in your hand, you will experience a sunny day and you will also close it accordingly well in the evening, thanking God, our eternal Father, and Christ, our Redeemer.

If the storm is still blowing, if the day is mixed, sometimes cloudy, sometimes sunny, then you will withdraw, if possible, for a few short, reflective minutes to think about what it actually means to be a Christian and what it means to be a servant of God.

To be a Christian means to give honor to God in all things. And to be a servant of God means to fulfill the will of our eternal Father step by step.

December 26

Draw strength by immersing in the very basis of the soul

If you want to open up the inner refuge and place of rest, practice immersing in your inner being, and thus learn to sink into the very basis of your soul.

There, in the stillness, in the peace, you will find rest. At the fountain of life, the love, you may draw strength, even during the course of a turbulent and hectic day, if now and then you can take a short break for a few minutes and withdraw to immerse in your inner being.

December 27

Immerse in the great, omnipresent love

The words of love are always valid. They are: Immerse in the great love. It is always present and helps.

December 28

Wisdom is not spiritual knowledge

Those who accumulate only spiritual knowledge remain spiritually blind. Nor do those who have accumulated a lot of spiritual knowledge still have the gift to distinguish between knowledge, wisdom and conscience.

However, those who have become wise by fulfilling the laws of the eternal Wisdom, GOD, have opened in themselves the All and behold the All. However, the knowledgeable ones merely speak of the All and nevertheless, remain their base self until they have overcome their base self, what restricts them and keeps them blind.

Take what has come close to you in wisdom, not only in your intellect—let it fall into your heart. Then it will move you again and again on this day, and you can counter your behavior with your heart's desire.

December 29

Create good starting conditions for the rest of your life

Hours of rest, of leisure are a refreshment for our soul as well as for our nervous system. A walk through the quiet, peaceful nature, an hour with a good book, with harmonious music, possibly also a quiet exchange among good friends or the like is food for the positive forces of the mind.

But also the movements in our day are good, when we use them to clear up possibly adverse circumstances. In this way, we create better starting conditions for our further life.

December 30

What do you make of this hour?

Perhaps you have time today to reflect on the following: At every hour, each of us is what we have made or are making of ourselves.

Who you were, who you are and who you will be, that lies in this, the present hour. Thus, this hour is a part of your past and also of your future, of your fate.

You are your past. What do you make of your past, of each hour? That is your future, your future fate.

December 31

Become a blessing for many

On this day you determine your future life, because how we shape our today will be our tomorrow.
Become a blessing for many through your selfless thoughts and actions!

Open Up and Find Yourself

The Treasure Chest of My Existence

Life's wisdom by Gabriele for your daily life. Simply take this small booklet in hand again and again. Let your consciousness choose the page... After all, there are no coincidences! So let yourself be surprised by what the day has in store for you.

"Each new morning is a small incarnation, a small new birth. Thus, each new day is a piece of a new life. We decide what we make of this day, ourselves."

144 pp., HB, Order No. S334en,
ISBN: 978-3-96446-262-6

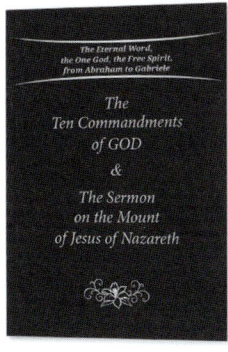

The Ten Commandments of GOD & The Sermon on the Mount of Jesus of Nazareth

Everything that we human beings need to live in peace with one another and in unity with nature and the animals, was already given to us thousands of years ago: They are the universal values that are contained for all people in the Ten Commandments of God and in the Sermon on the Mount of Jesus of Nazareth.

The Sermon on the Mount, however, is dismissed as utopian, and the Ten Commandments are changed or simply ignored as desired. Yet these fundamental principles have nothing to do with religions or churches. Rather, they are much more excerpts from the eternal law of the love for God and neighbor and apply to all people regardless of faith, culture or nationality. And one thing is very clear: They are not utopian, but quite livable, and lead to an inner peace and contentment and help us draw closer to God, the Free Spirit in us, step by step.

224 pp., HB, Order No. S182TBEN,
ISBN: 978-3-96446-264-0

We will be glad to send you
Our current catalog of books,
CDs and DVDs, as well as free excerpts
of our books on many different topics.

Gabriele Publishing House—The Word
P.O. Box 2221, Deering, NH 03244, USA
For North America, Toll-Free: 001-844-576-0937

or:

Max-Braun-St. 02, 97828 Marktheidenfeld, Germany
For international orders: +49.9391.504.843

www.gabriele-publishing-house.com